MANAGING TRADE RELATIONS IN THE NEW WORLD ECONOMY

Thomas Andersson

London and New York

To Ingrid

First published 1993
by Routledge
11 New Fetter Lane, London EC4P 4EE

Simultaneously published in the USA and Canada
by Routledge
29 West 35th Street, New York, NY 10001

© 1993 Thomas Andersson

Typeset in Garamond by
J&L Composition Ltd, Filey, North Yorkshire

Printed and bound in Great Britain by
Biddles Ltd, Guildford and King's Lynn

British Library Cataloguing in Publication Data

A catalogue record for this book is available from the British Library

ISBN 0–415–09568–9

Library of Congress Cataloging in Publication Data

Andersson, Thomas.
Managing trade relations in the New World economy /
Thomas Andersson.
p.   cm.
Simultaneously published in the USA and Canada.
Includes bibliographical references and index.
ISBN 0–415–09568–9
1. International trade. 2. Europe—Commerce—East Asia.
3. East Asia—Commerce—Europe.
4. East Asia—Economic integration.
I. Title.
HF1379.A53   1993
382′.09405—dc20   93–9831

CONTENTS

FIGURES

TABLES

FOREWORD

This book partly builds on *Europe and the East Asian Agenda*, Jean Monnet Chair Papers, published at the European University Institute, Florence, which is a joint work with Professor Staffan Burenstam Linder, President of the Stockholm School of Economics.

While the book covers a lot of ground, it does not claim to give full justice to all aspects which are touched upon, or to cover all strands of literature which are of relevance for the issues studied. The purpose is to provide a survey which synthesizes perspectives on some developments viewed as important for trade relations in the new world economy.

I am grateful for the valuable comments provided by my colleagues at the Industrial Institute for Economic and Social Research, Stockholm, and at the Stockholm School of Economics. In particular, I am indebted to Torbjörn Fredriksson, the Industrial Institute for Economic and Social Research, Stockholm, for excellent assistance. Thanks are also due to Nicklas Arvidsson and Håkan Hellström for their compilation of data. Financial support has been provided by the Swedish Research Council for the Humanities and Social Sciences.

Thomas Andersson

1

CHALLENGES OF A NEW ERA

A number of disconcerting developments have led to a change in the balance of power in international relations, and a replacement of the issues at the heart of the international agenda. This has involved a shift in the competition between geographical regions or economic systems. The second world of state planned economies has collapsed and ceased to exist as we knew it. Controlling resource use through central command has proved to be a hopelessly outdated mode of management. It is somewhat less evident that the first world – the industrialized and market-oriented economies of the West – has lost its formerly dominant position. The third world of developing countries, finally, has split into subcategories which display divergent economic trends.

Africa and most of South Asia face enormous economic problems. Above all, they are characterized by a state of poverty and stagnation that governs the lives of the majority of their rapidly growing populations. Irrespective of whether people remain in the countryside or move to the sprawling slums of the urban areas, there appears to be little escape. The Latin American and Caribbean experience is largely the same, although there are now encouraging signs of industrial progress in parts of the region.

East Asia, on the other hand, is characterized by a phenomenal dynamism, which stands out as a remarkable success story. The leading economy in this part of the world, Japan, has not only been transformed into a major industrialized nation, but has also become a global power in trade, investment and finance. Although affected by the weak state of the global economy in the early 1990s, its record is unlikely to be more than temporarily set back. While Japan so far remains dominant in East Asia in economic terms, the Asian newly-industrialized economies (ANIEs) are following closely behind. The members of the Association of South-East Asian Nations (ASEAN) have also recorded steady growth for several decades.[1] Poorer countries in the region are showing progress as well. This includes China itself, the world's most populous country which historically used to be the undisputed heart of Asia, in cultural as well as economic respects.

The turbulent changes in different regions have had repercussions on each other. The structure of the Soviet Union was eradicated by centrifugal forces, while the costs of trying to match the armaments of the United States speeded up the reappraisal of policies. Asian Pacific dynamism also played a role, exposing the lagging Soviet Union to unfavourable comparisons. A dynamic Far East, and not just a threatening West, undermined the relative strength of the economic base provided by the Soviet system for military security.

As the Cold War seems to be over, the ideological struggle between industrialized and developing countries has fewer military connotations. In the South, the image of a 'bloc' of exploited countries has started to fade. The doctrines upon which the third world based itself have become less relevant and less realistic. Foreign investors are now called for rather than resented, and the expropriation of foreign equity has virtually stopped. Export opportunities to industrialized countries are no longer viewed as signs of exploitation. Instead, evil is associated with the elimination of such opportunities.

Although foreign policies of appeasement and coexistence may be applied at less risk, security problems have not disappeared. Violent and dangerous conflicts are still occurring. However, military force has become a less viable and effective instrument for managing them. There are conspicuous exceptions, such as the Allied reply to Iraq's annexation of Kuwait. Most conflicts, such as those in Sri Lanka, Palestine or former Yugoslavia, to mention just a few, emanate from inner antagonisms, fuelled by economic and social tensions. Although the world community can undoubtedly still play a positive role in the resolution of such conflicts, specific measures now appear to require the support of broad international coalitions. At long last, the United Nations may fulfil a proper function in this respect.

The United States and the Soviet Union used to assume special roles on the basis of armed might. Now, military build-up has ceased to be a 'virtue', because of the costs of modern weaponry and the intensified pursuit of economic goals rather than ideological struggles across the world. The Russian Republic and the other 'heirs' of the USSR must dismantle obsolete structures and build new societies with small financial means and limited experience of functioning markets. While the area threatens to remain a source of destabilization for itself and for others, the only conceivable interference from outside is that of economic cooperation and assistance. Meanwhile, the previously undisputed leadership of the United States is now gone as a result of an inability to 'keep its own house in order' and correct its deficits, combined with the unavoidable relative decline as others grow.

Broadly speaking, national size no longer constitutes the advantage for growth that it used to. While 'bigness' can be effectively managed over the strategic or military dimension, it is not so easy over the social or economic one. Getting the Russian economy to work will not be facilitated by its dimensions – resource-rich economies in Africa and Latin America are among the most troubled, while the United States is in difficulty regarding its long-term vitality. The most successful economies are now relatively small. What matters is not a comfortable home market but the competitive pressure that follows from international exposure. Rewards do not first and foremost emanate from dominance at home or a rich endowment of natural resources, but rather from technology, high quality of human resources, knowledge and the ability to handle information.

Some observers see 'new' sources of conflict around the corner. History reminds us that, unfortunately, there is a tradition here. The ultimate wishes of Berlin and Tokyo might still be unclear. Their renewed ambitions point towards permanent seats in the Security Council of the United Nations, alongside those who were appointed after the Second World War. Unable to bring an independent foreign policy into military might, Germany and Japan have concentrated their energies on economic pursuits. This has again provided them with the means, if they should so desire, to widen their foreign policy into military might. Or have they found that the goals of foreign policy are better achieved through trade and investment than through diplomacy and the power to pursue the ultimate stage of diplomacy?

In fact, economic issues have replaced a concern for military security at the core of the international agenda. Japan and a reunited Germany are centres of the two regions that attract increasing attention. Questions are raised everywhere regarding how to counter the new competition from East Asia, and how to respond to the opportunities arising there. The Western economies are experiencing substantial trade deficits, particularly with Japan, but also with the ANIEs and China. It has become crucial to understand why East Asia has taken off, and to what extent it is possible to emulate, or learn from, its performance.

Germany, on the other hand, is the economic heavy-weight of the European Community (EC), and of Europe in general. Plagued by a severe economic and cultural segmentation between its many small national economies, Europe was for long a continent associated mainly with the past. Its firms have been too small to take full account of economies of scale, but too large for their national economies, resulting in high market concentration and monopolistic behaviour. Under growing external pressure, however, the French Commissioner Jacques Delors set off a major process of restructuring. The project of creating a 'Single Market', providing 'full freedom' for goods, services, capital and labour through the adoption of more than 300 common European laws, was planned for completion at the end of 1992. The door was opened to a new and potentially stronger Europe.

The Single Market is not the end of European integration. It is possible that the European Economic Area (EEA) will link most of the Western European 'outsiders' to the Single Market. Without means to influence the policies of the Community within that framework, however, it would appear that at least Sweden, Austria and Finland may be heading for membership. The process of restructuring has rapidly taken on additional dimensions within the EC itself. The weight of the unified Germany has created a strong drive to forge it into an even more united and secure Community. The changing and less stable international arena has raised demands for political and monetary unification as well.

In 1991 these movements were abruptly transformed into the Treaty of Maastricht. This has been countered by national and provincial concerns. The first act of popular consultation – the national referendum in Denmark – did not pass the test. Although the referendums in Ireland and France managed somewhat better, the integration process has become less predictable. Europe has been damaged by economic turbulence partly unleashed by the hardships and tensions resulting from German unification. Volatile exchange rates and excessive interest rates have become commonplace, business is suffering and unemployment, already high, is growing again.

4

While Western Europe must yet again take a closer look at how to manage its internal structure, Eastern Europe has problems to even get started. As sweeping changes are introduced in order to open up and transform the economies, formerly repressed incongruities and ethnic conflicts keep emerging. Being the largest capital-goods exporter in Europe, and also because of cultural and structural ties, Germany should eventually benefit the most from economic revitalization in Eastern Europe. On the other hand, it may have the most to lose from continued, and possibly even enlarged, turmoil.

The attempts to consolidate the European house have counterparts in processes towards regional integration elsewhere. The North American Free Trade Agreement (NAFTA) is planned to establish free trade between the United States, Canada and Mexico from 1994. Various constellations of developing countries are moving in the same direction. While East Asia fears that such regional constructs mainly intend to exclude its exports and investments, there are now conscientious efforts to establish more open exchange and cooperation in the Asian Pacific as well. This is becoming less unrealistic as the growing and maturing economies in the region become more compatible with each other. Hence, there is a widespread fear that the world economy will become segmented into 'blocs' of countries which liberalize trade amongst themselves but pursue protectionist policies *vis-à-vis* each other.[2]

The risk of segmentation of world markets does not stem from regional liberalization *per se*, but rather from a weakening of the multilateral trade system. After the Second World War, the General Agreement on Tariffs and Trade (GATT) established rules for world trade based on the principle of multilateralism – a country should not do against one of its trade partners what it does not do to all of them. For decades, trade and incomes grew steadily in the industrialized economies. Following the overhaul of the Bretton Woods system of fixed exchange rates, the 'oil crises' of the 1970s and the rise of new competitors, the world economy entered a phase of greater uncertainty and instability.

Parallel to these developments, business operations are characterized by rapid internationalization. Previously national firms have expanded into multinational enterprises that control affiliates in foreign markets through so-called foreign direct investment. Traditional trade in dissimilar products between countries with sharply different comparative advantages has given way to trade in differentiated products within industries, and even within firms, between countries which are highly similar. This trade is based primarily on technology and human skills, and specialization occurs in the form of quality or design. A relatively small number of giant corporations now operate intricate networks of transactions across national boundaries. Some flows are associated with a tangible, lasting restructuring. Other flows are completely flexible and occur with minimal time delay. Huge financial transactions are completed within minutes or seconds.

From the viewpoint of nation states, the internationalization process disentangles firms from their national bases. The financial and organizational capabilities of multinational firms, together with their weight in technology, production and trade, grant a capacity to circumvent requirements set up by individual governments. Workers and households are becoming more adaptive and mobile as well. Many regulations and controls are becoming less viable and more costly, which does not necessarily mean that they are dismantled. Governments throughout the world experience mounting difficulties in manoeuvring economies through financial or monetary policies.

From the standpoint of multinational firms, operations need to be organized in accordance with the special advantages of different locations. These hinge crucially on the actions of other players with which a firm interacts, private as well as public, and how they relate to the firm's needs and abilities. Activities based on advanced technology are particularly demanding with respect to inputs from outside, in the form of an appropriate infrastructure, an adequate work force, and proximity to other innovating units. Both firms and countries are confronted with strategic decisions. Which technology should be developed and which should be purchased or acquired? Which activities ought to be located in which markets? What skills should be promoted in the work force, and how? These circumstances generate an intensified interaction between actors on the national as well as international level, speeding up competition between locations, and between economic 'systems'.

The changing international scene accounts for many controversial issues with which the Uruguay Round of multilateral negotiations has battled for years. In the meantime, the old set of rules continues to hold, but is gradually becoming obsolete. Above all, the United States has adjusted its trade and investment policy, and has ceased to be constructive from a multilateral perspective. Many Americans accuse East Asian countries, particularly Japan, of unfair policies, while the United States itself has developed selective barriers at home. For example, 'Super 301' and 'Regular 301' have emerged as powerful bilateral instruments to bypass GATT requirements. Still, the inflexibility of the EC with respect to its agricultural policies has carried the major responsibility for the stalemate of the Uruguay Round. Following the United States, the EC has also developed a powerful agenda of voluntary export restraints and antidumping proceedings to selectively and arbitrarily impede competitive imports.

As old champions of free trade try on new clothes, and new ones are not yet fully dressed, there is a lack of *haute couture*. The tactical prowess which can be mobilized on a bilateral or regional basis threatens to determine the conditions for trade and the prospects of nations. With a diminished role for the United States in the world economy, the major question now is what paths will be chosen by Europe and East Asia. More specifically, how will these regions behave with regard to each other?

In the 1960s, Servan-Schreiber warned against American dominance over European industries. The advancement of East Asia, especially the Japanese, gives rise to similar concerns today. While the EC is preoccupied by its own restructuring, East Asian firms have expanded their efforts to be successful in this part of the world. For various reasons, many Europeans view their competition as damaging. Some react against the Japanese capturing of high technology segments that are of strategic importance. Others worry that the ANIEs or ASEAN will dominate activities based on medium technology. At the same time, European firms are often unwilling to make efforts within the markets of East Asia.

The external policy of the EC remains uncertain. This is also partly true of the principles or forces which are to shape the Community in general. To what extent should unguided market forces prevail? Should active industrial policies be adopted, and which policies in that case? The lack of determination in these matters is related to the question of how Europe should respond to the challenge of East Asia.

Western economic thought since Adam Smith has been based on the understanding that market forces are the result of human desires and ambitions. John Maynard Keynes advocated a role for governments as coordinators when transactions get stuck, which led the way out of the economic turmoil of the 1930s. The negative experience of 'fine-tuning', coupled with the insight that policy

7

makers often look after their own 'selfish' objectives rather than social welfare, subsequently led to the denouncement of discretionary economic policies. Hayek opted for liberty, in the form of unconstrained freedom of choice for individuals, as the prime objective of society. The breakdown of the planned economies has been taken as further support for this perspective.

The fact is that the model of unchecked market forces and minimal public action is losing pace. However, those Western economies which have tried mixed regimes, guiding private markets through heavy intervention and provision of transfer payments, are facing equally severe problems. Most of these economies suffer from weaknesses in industrial production as well as macroeconomic conditions, while the public sector keeps growing. In East Asia, on the other hand, growth is virtually nowhere a product of non-interventionist government. In Japan, the powerful Ministry of International Trade and Industry (MITI) has undoubtedly been a planner and catalyst of the Japanese record. In Korea, the Ministry of Trade and Industry (MTI) has played a major role in the expansion of industrial exports. At the same time, economic progress throughout takes place in the private sector, where corporate networks rapidly transform technologies and innovations into highly demanded products. The prevailing structures have contributed to the revival of the ideas of Joseph Schumpeter, who highlighted the importance of dynamic progress and the mechanisms in knowledge creation which lay behind it. Furthermore, attention is increasingly paid to the handling of human resources in East Asia.

Beyond international economic competition and the conditions for commercial trade, there are other acutely pressing issues which require action on a wide scale. The shadow of poverty continues to plague mankind, and threatens to get out of hand in the years ahead. With meagre improvement, or none at all, in the living conditions that confront the majority of the world's population in third world countries, there is little hope of bringing down birth rates and managing the demographic transition. The growing number of human beings on Earth exerts mounting pressure on the natural resource base, especially in countries with only rudimentary markets and little technological progress in the efficiency of resource use.

The basis of our existence – the life-supporting functions of the world's vegetation, the atmosphere and water systems – partly constitutes common 'resources' for all countries. Actors in the market place cannot claim ownership of these functions. Proximity to 'indirectly' useful activities is beneficial while getting rid of waste and pollutants without having to pay for it is convenient. In the long term, however, bills pile up. The spiralling impact of our expanding economic activities on the world's environment may deprive future generations of valuable options and eventually reduce the quality of life below that enjoyed currently.

Many individuals, firms and countries are taking steps to deal with this situation, but preferences vary regarding the pace of action as well as the instruments to use. Some see business opportunities in 'green' technology, while others consider it as a threat. Environmental movements commonly argue in favour of barriers to commercial trade, which they view as a source of damage. While there are many instances in which trade undoubtedly damages the environment, barriers reduce incomes and cause friction between countries.

Summing up, changes are taking place among the key actors in the world economy. There has been a replacement of the issues at the front of the international agenda. We are entering an era of new challenges, opportunities and risks. There is a more general acceptance of the usefulness of functioning market forces, less military preoccupation and more favourable options for peaceful coexistence. At the same time, there is a lack of leadership, and of untainted principles. The United States has lost its formerly dominant position and Europe is involved in a major attempt to restructure itself. East Asia has launched an economic challenge led by an expansion of manufactured exports, based on human skills and effort. The Western economies are experiencing large trade deficits, and Japan has turned into a major source of international investment. While the multilateral trading system has weakened, there is substantial regional liberalization. The appropriate role of policy makers in the economy appears uncertain. Finally, there are issues calling for action by the world community, such as the demographic explosion in the third world and damage inflicted on the global environment.

How can, and should, the West respond? Which factors are to guide the exchange between peoples and individuals in the future? This book seeks answers to such questions with a special focus on the relations between Europe and East Asia. Looking at simple comparisons of trade and investment, it will be emphasized that the potential relationship between these regions is underexploited. The handling of this 'missing link' will exert a major impact on the future direction of international economic relations in general.

The book is organized as follows. Chapter 2 surveys the international trade of recent decades, and examines the shift in gravity that has taken place between the Atlantic and the Pacific. The role of active export promotion policies in East Asia is pointed out. The chapter ends with a discussion of the major global effects of East Asia's growth performance.

Chapter 3 is concerned with foreign investment and country characteristics, especially in Japan and the other countries in East Asia. The chapter first considers the nature of direct investment, and its interplay with national economies. A survey of the special characteristics of Japanese society and industrial organization emphasizes the role of human interaction, which more or less extends to East Asia as a whole. The last three sections review the internationalization of business operations within East Asia, Japanese direct investment in the West, and foreign direct investment in Japan.

The impact of East Asian dynamism on trade policies is dealt with in Chapter 4. Most of the discussion of protectionism focuses on the changed role of the United States. The attempts to open up the Japanese market are analysed. Following the elaboration of 'supergains' from trade, the chapter further studies international movements towards trade liberalization, including regional integration. Finally, there is an analysis of influences on the 'unmanaged trade' in non-commercial environmental effects.

Chapter 5 studies the third leg of the world triangle in trade and investments, namely the far from fully developed exchange between Europe and East Asia. Special attention is paid to the European integration process, and how this affects, and is affected by, the relations with East Asian countries. The role of Japanese direct investment in Europe is further examined, as well as the prevalence of missed opportunities for exchange, especially for Europeans in East Asia.

Chapter 6 discusses implications for policies. The first part addresses the international situation, while the second focuses on the need for a European policy *vis-à-vis* East Asia.

2

THE SHIFT IN GRAVITY

International economic relations have become considerably more uncertain and difficult to predict in recent decades. In the early 1970s, the Bretton Woods system of fixed exchange rates fell apart in the aftermath of military spending by the United States during the Vietnam War. Following a few years of halfhearted attempts to establish a new fixed exchange rate mechanism, the major currencies have floated against each other. Smaller countries have usually found some way to peg their exchange rate to a larger one, or to some appropriate basket of currencies. Apart from this, the 1970s saw the unleashing of the oil price shocks. The oil-producing countries had finally gained control over their production, and through OPEC they were able to form a cartel and raise prices.[1]

Figure 2.1 shows the annual growth in world trade in current values. As can be seen, the picture is dominated by the effects of the oil price shocks in 1973–4 and 1978–9. The nominal value of world trade increased by more than 40 per cent in one year during the first, and more than 25 per cent during the second. As can also be seen from Figure 2.1, world income, at 1985 prices, fell markedly in the years following both events. In the early 1980s, the value of trade declined, as did the rate of growth. Although both trade and incomes recovered somewhat in the 1980s, the trend has been weaker than we have been used to since the Second World War.

Parallel to these developments, substantial changes have taken place in the world's trade and investment flows. This chapter is primarily concerned with the composition and direction of trade in goods, particularly manufactures. The next chapter goes beyond the aggregated level, and considers industrial organization and the internationalization of business operations. In both these chapters the observed changes signal a shift in gravity in the world economy

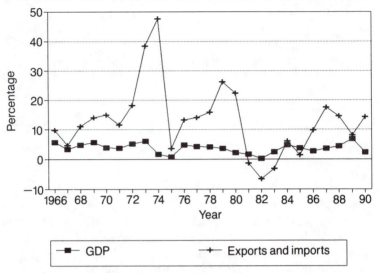

Figure 2.1 Real growth in world GDP (1985 prices) and nominal growth
in world trade, 1965–90 (per cent per annum)
Source: OECD 1991; United Nations, *International Trade Statistics Yearbook*,
various issues

which is much more profound than anything the oil price increases
could have achieved. Certain kinds of trade as well as certain regions
are expanding their roles, while others are declining in relative
importance. These developments are affecting the basic terms of
exchange.

2.1 SECTORAL AND INDUSTRIAL CHANGES IN INTERNATIONAL TRADE

Let us first survey how the sectoral and industrial composition of
trade has developed, before discussing the geographical reorientation. Studies undertaken in the early 1980s have emphasized the
increased role of fuels in world trade. As shown in Figure 2.2, the
jumps in oil prices had a major impact on the composition of trade.
The share of fuels in the total trade of goods expanded sharply
between 1970 and 1980, from 9 to 24 per cent, while all other
categories diminished in importance. Seen in a longer time perspective, however, the primacy of fuels was short. Its share of world
trade shrank in the 1980s, and had fallen to the level of 1970

12

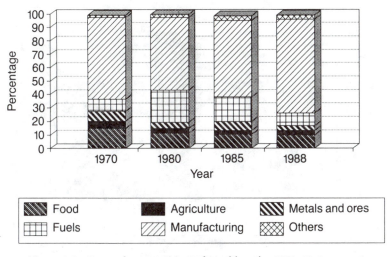

Figure 2.2 Sectoral composition of world trade, 1970–88 (per cent)
Source: UNCTAD 1987, 1990

by 1988. Meanwhile, both food and agricultural products have continued to lose ground, accounting for less than 10 per cent and less than 4 per cent of world trade respectively in 1988. Metals and ores increased their shares in the first half of the 1980s, but have subsequently declined.

The trade of manufactures, however, has not only retained but even surpassed the weight it had before the oil crises. In 1988, more than 70 per cent of the total trade in goods consisted of manufactures. This is not to say that the products traded in the world today are the same as twenty years ago. Breaking down the exports of manufactured products, Figure 2.3 shows an expansion for machinery and transport, electronic industries and, to some extent, chemicals. Iron and steel and other metals have contracted in relative terms. These industrial shifts indicate the change in the character of goods which has taken place within each industrial category.

The revived dominance of trade in manufactured products is sometimes downplayed by the expansion of services. Although there are insufficient data in this field, the international flows of finance and insurance in particular have taken on enormous dimensions. In addition, services have become intertwined with the production of goods. However, the emphasis on services reflects the advancement of the same fundamental source of growth as the

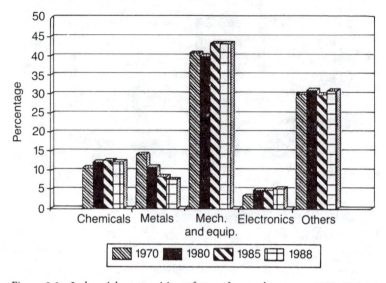

Figure 2.3 Industrial composition of manufactured exports, 1970–88 (per cent)

expansion of trade in manufactured products, and the changing weight of industries within manufacturing. Natural resources and low wages are becoming less important determinants of international trade and production patterns. The quality of skills in organization, insurance and finance, the undertaking and utilization of research and development (R&D), marketing and distribution, etc., are now crucial components in the value-added chain of all sorts of products. Such factors are increasingly dictating the direction of international trade flows, as well as the welfare of societies.

As will be further discussed in the next chapter, the nature of world trade is changing from inter-industry to intra-industry trade in differentiated products, and even to intra-firm trade. The latter is motivated by economies of scale and scope in production, imperfect competition, and consumers' taste for variety. Before further considering these issues, let us examine the major geographical shift in international economic relations.

2.2 THE RISE OF EAST ASIA

In Figure 2.4, manufactured exports from the OECD countries are categorized in terms of their distribution to major markets.[2] The main impression is of large fluctuations, which are associated with misalignments between the key exchange rates – the dollar, the yen and the Deutschmark. The share of the North American market shrank from a little more than 13 per cent in 1970 to 10 per cent in 1980, after which there was a revival to almost 19 per cent in the mid-1980s. By 1988, the North American market had again fallen to 15 per cent of OECD's manufactured exports. The share of the EC fluctuated as well, but in the opposite direction to the United States. After a declining trend in the early 1980s, the EC market grew in the late 1980s, reaching 43 per cent in 1988. Throughout, the EC was the largest destination for OECD's manufactured exports. It should be noted, however, that the comparison between the EC and the United States is biased as trade between EC countries is included while trade between American states is not. 'Other nations' diminished in importance, and regions with very poor countries, such as Africa, declined to an even greater extent. Japan's share was growing, but at a low level.

Figure 2.5 shows OECD's exports of manufactured products by exporters. Here, there is a consistent declining trend for the United States, and mostly an increase for Japan. The US share shrank from 17.5 per cent in 1970 to 14.2 per cent in 1988. At the

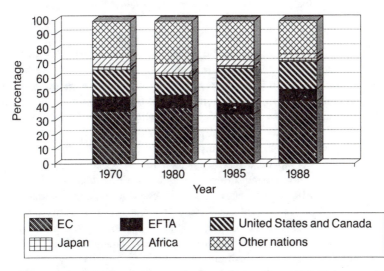

Figure 2.4 OECD manufactured exports by market, 1970–88 (per cent)
Source: UNCTAD 1987, 1990

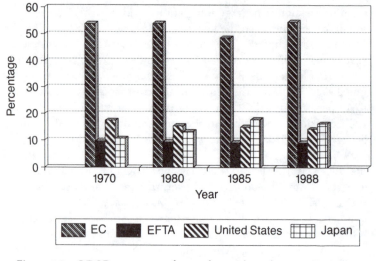

Figure 2.5 OECD exporters of manufactured products, 1970–88 (per cent)
Source: UNCTAD 1987, 1990

same time, Japan's share increased from 10 per cent to more than 16 per cent. The share of the EC became less enhanced in the first half of the 1980s, but had returned to its previous level of about 53 per cent in 1988.

These trends are roughly the same viewed from the perspective of the major industries. Throughout, Japanese exports advanced during most of the decade. The same could be said about the EC in the late 1980s, while the shares of the United States were reduced. In iron and steel as well as machinery and transport, the decline of the United States was well under way in the 1970s. In 'other metal products' and 'other industrial products', where the United States used to hold a stronger position, the downturn came in the 1980s. However, the Japanese have advanced in particular in industries characterized by strong international expansion. This applies to electronics, office equipment and data processing, while the chemicals sector is a partial exception. In the strategically important semiconductor market, for example, Japan's share surpassed that of the United States in the mid-1980s. As of 1991, Japan had six of the leading companies in the field, including the top two, while the United States had three and Europe one (Philips), which was down in tenth place.

In spite of the market shares lost by the United States, its export specialization within manufacturing has remained directed towards the rapidly expanding sectors, with electronics, data processing and chemicals among the major products. With regard to developments up to 1985, Buigues and Goybet (1989) noted that the EC, on the other hand, lost market shares in expanding sectors, and developed more favourably in relatively stagnant ones, such as leather, footwear and furniture. Especially compared with the Europeans, the Japanese have been flexible in orienting their efforts towards rapidly expanding sectors.

So far, we have only discussed the division within the OECD. Table 2.1 shows the share of manufactured exports provided by various groups of exporting countries, i.e. the OECD, the ANIEs, Eastern Europe, Socialist Asia and other developing countries. A paramount success has been recorded for the ANIEs. Their share of the world's manufactured exports more than doubled in the 1970s, and increased by more than 70 per cent between 1980 and 1988. Among other developing countries, the greatest increase occurred in Southeast Asia during this period. The OECD was able to maintain its predominant position in industrial exports in the 1970s, as the 'four tigers' advanced mainly at the expense of Eastern Europe. Between 1980 and 1988, however, OECD's share diminished from 82 per cent to 77 per cent. The decline was particularly large in iron and steel, where it fell from 85 per cent to 75 per cent. In machinery and transport, OECD regressed from about 85 per cent to 82 per cent, while the four tigers and other developing countries increased from 2 per cent to more than 11 per cent.

The expansion of manufactured exports achieved by the ANIEs has had a significant impact on the sales of almost all industrial goods' categories in practically all major markets. With only about 70 million inhabitants altogether, they account for some 70 per cent of all exports of manufactured goods from developing countries. Of

Table 2.1 Exporters of manufactured products, per cent, 1970–88

Year	OECD	ANIEs	Eastern Europe	Socialist Asia	Other developing countries
1970	83.0	2.0	9.3	0.6	5.0
1980	82.5	4.8	7.0	0.9	4.8
1985	79.4	6.8	5.9	1.0	6.9
1988	77.3	8.2	5.7	1.3	7.6

Source: UNCTAD 1987, 1990

course, the change has varied in different industries and countries. Nevertheless, in the early 1980s, the four ANIEs had already achieved a larger import penetration ratio[3] than the Latin American NIEs Mexico and Brazil in all OECD countries except Italy (OECD 1988).

Table 2.2 demonstrates the advancement of these six NIEs together in the major EC markets, the United States, Australia, Japan and Sweden between 1970 and 1985. Figures are given for total manufactures, textiles, electrical machinery and appliances, and communication. The NIEs recorded a significant increase in all EC countries in all these product groups, as well as in total manufacturing. There was even more progress in the United States, Australia and Sweden, while there was much less in Japan. Broadly speaking, the highest ratios were recorded in textiles, followed by radio and television.

What we are witnessing is a rise of East Asia in economic terms which is of historical dimensions. East Asia is here understood to include Japan, the four ANIEs and the ASEAN. The Asian Pacific region also incorporates Australia, New Zealand, Papua New Guinea and the island states of the South Pacific. The whole Pacific Basin includes China and the Canadian and US western seaboard states. Of course, Indochina, Burma and the Democratic Republic of Korea are part of this region in practice, but have here been left out of the statistics.

Table 2.2 Import penetration ratios, total for newly industrialized economies, 1970 and 1985 (per cent)

Countries	Product groups							
	Total manufactures		Textiles, clothing, leather, footwear		Electrical machinery and appliances		Radio and television	
	1970	1985	1970	1985	1970	1985	1970	1985
United States	0.49	2.41	1.53	11.16	0.44	5.93	1.55	7.54
Japan	0.30	0.85	1.17	3.82	0.10	0.73	0.19	0.68
Germany, Federal Republic	0.38	1.40	1.33	7.96	0.04	1.32	0.38	5.36
France	0.15	0.79	0.11	2.08	0.01	0.73	0.06	2.39
UK	0.41	1.42	2.10	7.74	0.14	1.15	0.37	4.11
Italy	0.27	0.91	0.34	1.18	0.07	0.52	0.40	3.91
Sweden	0.65	1.80	4.03	18.72	0.02	1.09	0.20	5.31

Source: OECD 1988

In several respects, the Pacific Basin will no doubt have overtaken the Atlantic Basin by the year 2000. To some extent, this gravity shift has already taken place. Table 2.3 presents basic data on population, area, gross domestic product (GDP) and GDP per capita for the countries in the Pacific Basin. The dominance of Japan in economic terms is evident. In fact, the country's GDP accounts for some 55 per cent of total GDP of the entire Pacific Basin. China, with the second largest economy of the Asian countries, is even more predominant in terms of population. It should be recalled, however, that inter-country comparisons of national income are biased in various respects. In the case of China, national income is markedly underestimated because of the undervaluation of the yuan. Looking at industrial production or . commercial exports, the country's income is undoubtedly several times larger than reported in the official statistics. Thus, Japan's economic dominance in East Asia is not quite as pronounced as it appears.

Table 2.4 presents the shares of Asian Pacific countries in world population and world area, as well as the size of income relative to the total for the OECD. East Asia accounts for some 10 per cent of the world's population and less than 4 per cent of its area, while

Table 2.3 Population, area and income of Pacific Basin countries, 1990

Region	Population (millions)	Area (1,000 km²)	GDP (billion US$)	GNP/capita (US$)
Japan	123.6	378	2,940	23,960
Korea	42.8	98	244	5,660
Taiwan	20.4	36	156	7,990
Hong Kong	6	1	63[a]	10,300[a]
Singapore	3	1	35	11,750
Malaysia	17.9	330	42	2,270
Thailand	57.2	514	80	1,390
Indonesia	179.3	1,905	107	570
Philippines	61.5	300	44	720
Papua New Guinea	3.7	462	3.2	900
Australia	17.1	7,687	296	16,500
New Zealand	3.4	269	44	12,460
China	1,133.7	9,561	336[a]	330
US Pacific states	38.3	2,368	692	14,570

Sources: International Monetary Fund 1992; Europa 1991, 1992; Department of Commerce 1991; Statistics of Sweden 1991
Note: [a] 1989.

19

its income corresponds to 23 per cent of the total for the OECD. With the inclusion of Australia, the Asian Pacific region holds more than 12 per cent of the world's land area. The Pacific Basin contains 32 per cent of the world's population, almost 25 per cent of its area and 31 per cent relative to the income of the OECD. The United States and the European OECD countries are much smaller in terms of population and area, while their shares of income are slightly larger. If the entire Pacific Basin was put to use as effectively as East Asia, the income of the OECD would be dwarfed in comparison.

Table 2.4 Shares of various Asian Pacific countries and groupings, and of the United States, Europe (OECD), Asian Pacific region and China, in world population, area and OECD income, 1990

	Population (% of world total)	Area (% of world total)	GDP (% of total OECD)
Japan	2.4	0.4	18.1
ASEAN	6.1	3.2	1.9
ANIEs	1.3	0.1	3.0
East Asia	9.8	3.7	23.0
Asian Pacific region	10.1	12.4	24.9
China	21.6	9.9	2.2
US Pacific states	0.8	2.5	4.3
Total Pacific Basin	32.4	24.8	31.4
United States	4.8	9.7	33.2
Europe (OECD)	6.9	4.4	43.0

Source: See Table 2.3

The development of East Asia's GDP relative to those of the OECD, the United States and OECD Europe is shown in Table 2.5. Japan's share almost doubled from 1970 to 1990, reaching 18 per cent of the OECD's income in the latter year. The relative income of the ANIEs increased as much as three times, while ASEAN lost some ground in the late 1980s. Relative to the United States, the weight of the East Asian countries increased to an even greater extent, although the United States temporarily regained some momentum in the early 1980s with the rising dollar. The increase relative to OECD Europe was smaller owing to the higher growth here compared with the United States. The income of East Asia as a whole was equivalent to 70 per cent of total US income in 1990, and some 53 per cent in comparison with OECD Europe. In spite of the stronger European record in the latter half of the

Table 2.5 Various GDP ratios, 1970–90 (per cent)

Ratios	1970	1980	1985	1990
Japan GDP over				
OECD GDP	9.5	13.8	15.1	18.1
ANIEs GDP over				
OECD GDP	1.0	1.8	2.4	3.0
ASEAN GDP over				
OECD GDP	1.5	2.2	2.4	1.9
Japan GDP over				
US GDP	20.0	40.2	33.5	54.5
ANIEs GDP over				
US GDP	2.0	5.4	5.3	9.0
ASEAN GDP over				
US GDP	3.2	6.5	5.4	5.6
Japan GDP over				
OECD Europe GDP	25.4	29.7	45.0	42.1
ANIEs GDP over				
OECD Europe GDP	2.5	4.0	7.1	7.0
ASEAN GDP over				
OECD Europe GDP	4.1	4.8	7.2	4.3

Sources: International Monetary Fund 1991; OECD, *Main Economic Indicators,* various issues

decade, incomes grew more than twice as fast in East Asia as in the rest of the world in the 1980s. Even if there is some slowdown ahead, a major revival of trends is needed if East Asia is not to overtake both North America and Western Europe a few years into the next century. The gravity shift is even more marked when China is considered as well. According to some forecasts, China will have become the world's largest single economy by the year 2010.[4]

The pace of change is still greater in exports, however. For the Asian Pacific region, Table 2.6 indicates that its share of world exports increased from 9 per cent in 1960 to 22 per cent in 1988. Compared with US trade, that of the Asian Pacific grew from less than 70 per cent to more than 140 per cent between these years. US trade with the Asian Pacific region had surpassed US trade with Europe by 1980, and was 40 per cent larger in 1988. In this year, EC trade with the Asian Pacific region grew to almost the same size as EC trade with the United States. In fact, the *US–EC* link became the smallest in the first six months of 1991 (ITC 1992). As can be seen in Table 2.7, the United States mostly accounted for a growing share of the total exports from the Asian Pacific

Table 2.6 Changes in Asian Pacific trade flow ratios, 1960–88 (per cent)

Ratios	1960	1970	1980	1985	1987	1988
Exports: Asian Pacific over world	9.0	12.9	15.3	20.3	21.1	22.1
Manufactured exports: Asian Pacific over world	8.7	14.2	19.9	23.2	23.4	n.a.
Trade: Asian Pacific over US	69.7	87.8	121.9	117.2	130.9	140.0
Trade: Asian Pacific over European (OECD)	23.1	26.8	34.4	43.2	39.0	43.1
Trade: Asian Pacific over European (OECD) (excl. intra-European)	36.5	n.a.	62.3	n.a.	n.a.	90.1
Asian Pacific trade over trade of LDCs	43.2	68.8	50.5	65.3	74.7	73.1
US trade with Asian Pacific over US trade with Europe (OECD)	48.1	70.8	97.8	125.2	135.0	139.3
EC trade with Asian Pacific over EC trade with United States	60.8	49.2	68.6	62.3	88.1	96.8
Trade of Asian Pacific LDCs over trade of the other LDCs	21.7	30.0	28.8	42.6	57.7	59.5
Manufactured exports of Asian Pacific LDCs over total manufactured exports of all LDCs	30.9	41.6	64.3	72.9	74.2	n.a.
Manufactured exports: Asian Pacific NIEs over exports of all LDCs	24.2	36.2	56.2	64.7	66.8	n.a.

Sources: International Monetary Fund, *Directory of Trade Statistics*, various issues; Republic of China, *Taiwan Statistical Data Book*, various issues
Notes: LDC, less developed country; n.a., not available.

until 1987, while Western and Eastern Europe, as well as developing countries in other regions, diminished in importance.

The most commonly discussed aspects of the reorientation in trade are the US and EC deficits with Japan, which have been growing fairly steadily for two decades. Figure 2.6 shows the consistent widening between the value of exports and imports *vis-à-vis* Japan. In the 1980s, substantial imbalances emerged with the ANIEs and China as well. Throughout the twentieth century, the United States has had much more exchange with East Asia than has Europe, and a considerably larger deficit in absolute terms.[5] It is not only the size of the deficits which is bothersome, however, but

Table 2.7 Exports from the Asian Pacific region to principal importing countries and country groups as a percentage of total Asian Pacific exports, 1960–88

Country	1960	1970	1980	1985	1987	1988
United States	18.5	26.8	22.5	29.5	32.6	29.7
Canada	1.8	2.6	1.6	2.1	2.2	2.1
Europe (OECD)	24.7	17.7	16.5	13.7	18.0	18.6
Non-Asian Pacific LDCs (excl. China)	16.3	12.0	16.2	11.6	9.6	10.0
China	0.8	2.1	2.8	6.1	4.6	5.1
USSR, Eastern Europe	2.6	2.2	2.4	1.4	0.9	0.9
Asian Pacific Countries	26.5	32.5	36.2	30.5	31.2	33.5
Total	91.2	95.9	98.2	94.9	99.1	99.9

Source: See Table 2.6

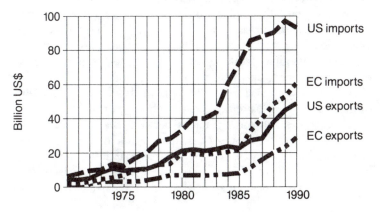

Figure 2.6 US and EC trade with Japan, 1970–90
Source: International Monetary Fund 1991

their composition as well. Looking at US–Japanese trade, for example, the United States exports predominantly wheat, soybeans, lumber and aircraft. In the other direction, trade consists of robots, telecommunications equipment, computers and semiconductors.

East Asia is not on level terms with the West in all respects. The United States dominates in R&D, where it accounted for almost half the world's total as of the mid-1980s. The United States has by far the largest 'exports' in this field, measured on the basis of royalty payments. At the same time, the United States is the only country in which the public sector is the leading investor in R&D. In the OECD as a whole, some two-thirds of all R&D was undertaken by private industry. American companies made the leading efforts in virtually all industries, as seen from Table 2.8. The United States was particularly dominant in aerospace and machinery, and was the least ahead in services and metals. The EC accounted for only about one-quarter of all R&D, and its share was shrinking during the 1980s. The most expansive countries in this respect have been Japan and small West European countries like Sweden and Switzerland. Relative to value added, these three countries had the highest R&D intensity as of the mid-1980s (OECD 1989).

As we have seen already, the US position in R&D is not altogether reflected in the trade of goods. Obviously, R&D is merely one step in the production process. Converting new knowledge to commercially useful activities is another thing. In spite of the modest domestic emphasis on R&D and its great advancement in R&D-intensive production, Japan has achieved a balance in its international payments for technology, as measured on the basis of royalties. These issues will be returned to in the ensuing chapters.

Briefly summing up these two sections, world trade has shifted towards activities based primarily on human skills and technology. In the geographical pattern, there have been great fluctuations due to the oil crises and misalignments between the main currencies. Underlying these trends is a consistent decline of the US share of manufactured exports. While the EC has manifested itself as the largest player in world trade, the major change consists of the remarkable export performance achieved by Japan and the ANIEs.

Table 2.8 Estimated shares in OECD total research and development in various industries, 1983 (per cent)

Industry	United States	Japan	EC	Others
Electrical/electronics	47.4	18.1	26.5	8.0
Machinery	61.1	13.6	17.5	7.8
Aerospace	77.8	0.0	19.4	2.7
Other transport	43.3	23.8	27.0	5.9
Metals	33.7	29.1	25.3	11.9
Chemicals	43.7	16.5	29.9	9.9
Chemicals-linked	39.4	25.8	25.3	9.5
Services	29.7	20.7	26.4	23.3
Business sector as a whole	51.3	16.0	26.7	6.0

Source: OECD 1989

Both the United States and the EC have experienced growing trade deficits with Japan for about two decades. Finally, we have noted that the United States has a predominant position in R&D, while the EC's share is diminishing. Japan's share of R&D is growing but still at a fairly low level, and does not match the country's advancement in products based on high technology.

2.3 ACTIVE EXPORT ORIENTATION

There are many views of what has spurred the phenomenal development in East Asia. Some have focused on factors that are unique to the region. Such *ad hoc* explanations include references to Confucian values, the economic skills of the Chinese and Chinese minorities, the Japanese ethos, the industriousness of the labour force and the high level of education, lack of raw materials, abundant United States aid, political stability and so forth.

There are considerable merits to several of these explanations, and some will be further dealt with later. Still, a basic problem with them all is their *ad hoc* nature. The region is heterogeneous in every way, with countries differing in history, constitution, race, size, resource endowments and climate. Yet, high growth is the typical pattern in the countries here referred to as East Asia. Indochina, Burma and North Korea display a very different record. China itself made impressive progress from 1979 onwards. Although it set itself back with the retreat from economic reforms after the events in Tiananmen Square in 1989, there is again an acceptance of market mechanisms, and China's economic prospects have resumed in the early 1990s.

While the specific design of policies differs across countries, those that have succeeded share certain basic characteristics. The most clearcut and general difference compared with the third world as a whole is that East Asia has pursued relatively more export-oriented policies. Governments have promoted sales on world markets, exposure to competition and utilization of scale advantages, while other developing countries have rather tended to bias their incentive systems away from world markets and comparative advantage. Considerably smaller price distortions have been found in East Asia compared with most other developing countries (World Bank 1983).

In fact, the level of development in the individual countries in East Asia fairly well reflects the dates at which they embraced export-oriented policies. In Japan, the beginning was marked by the Meiji restoration in 1868. South Korea and Taiwan took the crucial steps in the early 1960s, and Thailand in the early 1980s. The Philippines has not yet made any equally conscious turn in this direction, and its development record is weak. These systematic differences in performance point towards a major influence of economic policies. Little (1981) concluded that the success of the ANIEs is entirely due to 'good policies and the people'. These are related explanations. 'Good people' have pursued good policies, and good polices have been facilitated by 'good people'.

This is not to say that the East Asian countries, with the exception of Hong Kong, have practised *laissez faire*. Export promotion has not taken place through a general liberalization of imports. Instead, exchange rate management has been combined with fiscal incentives for exports. The overriding objective has been to secure macroeconomic stability, however. Budgets have been kept in balance, which has contributed to high savings and low inflation. Nominal exchange rates have been adjusted in order to keep real exchange rates at reasonable levels. Sound public finances have allowed promotion of industrial growth without excessive taxation of agriculture, which has instead been protected relative to industry (Sachs 1986).

The involvement of governments in the management of private industries is harder to evaluate. Korea, for example, has supplemented selective export promotion with more than moderate protectionism. It is true that the result has been roughly neutrality on the whole, but the government has still played a major role in selecting which sectors should be expanded. At the same time, private initiatives and ownership have been at the core of the development process. It is true that the state-owned companies are not particularly 'small' in East Asia, compared with, for example, Latin America. Nevertheless, their share of industry is small relative to that of the private sector, and their growth has been low throughout, with the exception of the oil sector in Indonesia (Riedel 1988).

Whether economic performance would have been even better without active government support of certain activities it is difficult to know. However, the measures used have generally aimed to stimulate the efficiency of the private sector. Incentives have promoted activities thought to be, or to be capable of becoming, in line with comparative advantage, at one point labour intensity, at another capital intensity. Input and output prices have been carefully maintained at the level of the world market, in order to encourage competition.

The successful export-led growth in East Asia has affected the rest of the world in a number of ways. Before tracing the sources of growth further, the rest of this chapter surveys some of the influences. Three effects are distinguished: (a) the demonstration effect, (b) the opportunity of a larger world, and (c) the threat to established interests.

2.4 THE DEMONSTRATION EFFECT

Growth explained by reference to a set of policies may be possible to duplicate. The image of a growth 'miracle' is displaced by that of a growth 'model'. The fact that there are many differences between the East Asian countries lends support to the idea that others can replicate their performance. A resemblance to the policies originally favoured by the West in the early phases of industrialization further stimulates this reasoning: It can be repeated – you can do it too!

The demonstration effect has already had considerable influence on the policies of other developing countries. Although some countries will continue to be poor because of gravely inhospitable conditions, it has become obvious that many contribute to their own economic and social debacle by inept, not to say disastrous, economic policies. There is now much less call for a New World Economic Order – with 'massive resource transfers' coupled with regulated international trade and prices. The requirements for resource transfers are instead becoming associated with the lack of functioning markets with regard to common property issues.

There are various attempts to emulate the East Asian example. These encompass steps that both allow markets to determine prices in previously planned economies and expose protected economies to competition from world markets. It has already been noted that China is again moving in this direction, no doubt spurred by the striking differences in performance. Vietnam and Laos have pursued economic reforms at an even greater pace, and both countries have experienced some improvement in economic conditions. After having managed to establish at least moderately stable democracies, most of Latin America is following a similar track. The pace of change is still slow in many countries, however, particularly in Africa.

There is now little doubt concerning the virtues of the export-oriented growth strategy as far as East Asia itself is concerned, but objections are still raised about its viability for others. It has been argued, for example, that reliance on exports makes developing countries dependent on growth in the industrialized countries, so that the former do well only when the latter do. This argument is effectively countered by the rapid growth of market shares that the ANIEs have been able to achieve in industrialized economies.

Another more biting counterargument to export orientation may be referred to as the 'adding-up' problem. The fierceness with which Japan and the ANIEs have already penetrated the markets of the industrialized countries has been met with accusations of unfair trade behaviour. There are now plenty of quantitative restrictions protecting industries. Since the late 1970s, many developed countries have assigned a global market share to the developing world in general and then distributed quotas for individual countries within that global quota. With an increasing number of developing countries competing for industrial exports, the protectionist barrier is mounting for individual exporters. Thus, the traditional elasticity pessimism of those in favour of import substitution has been replaced by a new one, based on the protectionist measures applied against producers in poor countries.

Some factors suggest that the difficulties facing other developing countries who follow East Asia on the track of export orientation are exaggerated. Greater exports lead to increased purchasing capacity and larger imports. Hence, there will not necessarily be any larger deficits for the industrialized countries, but simply more trade. As some currently poor countries reach a higher level of development, and their costs rise, the less developed countries become more competitive. In addition, there are improved possibilities for trade between third world countries as they grow at a different pace and become more complementary in nature. This trend is the most evident within East Asia, where we have already noted the strong growth in intra-regional trade.

However, the problems of protectionism cannot be easily dismissed. There is no doubt that such policies do limit the growth of exports. The most noticeable examples are agricultural products, and clothing and textiles. It is no coincidence that these goods' categories, in which countries with low labour costs generally have their most clearcut comparative advantage, are plagued by the most severe non-tariff barriers to trade. For decades, they were removed from the ordinary agenda of multilateral trade negotiations because they were politically sensitive for the governments in the EC and Japan. When the agricultural policies were eventually addressed, mostly because the subsidies and barriers had become painful for the United States, the multilateral trade talks became paralysed.

It is far from straightforward to evaluate the new elasticity pessimism, as the course and impact of protectionism will depend on the whole framework of international trade arrangements. As will be further analysed in subsequent chapters, we currently have strong tendencies towards both protectionism and liberalization in the world economy. In any case, the uncertainty which prevails with respect to the future accessibility of the markets of industrialized countries seriously reduces the strength of the demonstration effect among policy makers in the third world.

The demonstration effect has under all circumstances had a profound impact on economic and philosophic lines of thought. Concerning development theory, neo-Marxism and the 'dependency' school of 'unequal exchange' have expired. The traditional import substitution school argued that secularly falling terms of trade and limited markets would make it impossible for developing countries to rely on exports.[6] The fact is, however, that it is precisely those countries which have gone for the world market that have succeeded in achieving development. The foundation of Marxian and neo-Marxian theory has similarly been undercut. The *Communist Manifesto* shows that Marx looked upon capitalism as a powerful engine of growth which would spread to the poor countries and lead to an expansion of output there as well. Its breakdown would come later because of the inner contradictions of strong capitalist growth. It was neo-Marxists, impatient with the downfall of capitalism and unwilling to experience capitalism in developing countries, who formed the arguments of exploitation of poor countries.

There are demonstration effects on neoclassical economics as well. East Asian dynamism has not only added new insights into the virtues of market forces, but has also demonstrated that governments can actively intervene in the operations of markets without necessarily spoiling the prospects for growth and development. In addition, new attention is paid to other factors, such as the role of information, investment in human skills and the nature of competition or cooperation. The question has been raised whether Japan and the other countries in East Asia are playing the capitalist game on terms which are inherently different from those practised by the market economies of the West. These issues will be extensively discussed in subsequent chapters.

2.5 THE OPPORTUNITY OF A LARGER WORLD

The Asian Pacific has not only become more important in trade as a result of its increased exports. As shown in Table 2.9, imports have grown dramatically as well. For example, the region's imports from the United States have expanded from US$3 billion in 1960 to US$98 billion in 1988. In the same period, imports from Europe rose from US$3 billion to US$83 billion. Nonetheless, the American and European market shares in the Asian Pacific have generally declined, as can be seen in the lower part of the table. The reason is that intra-regional trade has grown fast enough for practically all market shares of external regions to diminish. East Asia contains without comparison the world's most rapidly expanding markets.

Table 2.9 Imports of the Asian Pacific region from principal countries and country groups, 1960–88 (billion US$)

Country	1960	1970	1980	1985	1987	1988
United States	2.9	9.4	51.9	56.5	70.8	98.0
Canada	0.4	1.3	6.8	7.2	9.5	12.8
Europe (OECD)	2.9	6.8	33.4	41.1	64.1	82.6
Non-Asian Pacific LDCs						
(excl. China)	1.7	6.6	90.0	53.1	39.8	62.9
China	0.4	1.0	10.8	17.7	25.8	34.1
USSR, Eastern Europe	0.1	0.9	3.0	2.0	3.5	4.5
Asian Pacific countries	3.6	12.2	87.7	114.9	155.7	196.8
Total	12.0	38.2	283.6	305.6	369.2	491.7
Percentage of total Asian Pacific imports						
United States	22.5	24.1	17.5	18.5	18.3	19.8
Canada	2.8	3.3	2.3	2.4	2.5	2.6
Europe (OECD)	22.1	17.6	11.3	13.4	16.6	16.7
Non-Asian Pacific LDCs						
(excl. China)	12.9	17.1	30.4	17.0	10.3	12.7
China	2.8	2.6	3.6	5.8	6.6	6.9
USSR, Eastern Europe	1.1	2.3	1.0	0.7	0.9	0.9
Asian Pacific countries	28.4	31.6	29.6	37.6	40.3	39.8
Total	92.6	98.6	95.7	95.4	95.5	99.4

Sources: International Monetary Fund, *Directory of Trade Statistics*, various issues; Republic of China, *Taiwan Statistical Data Book*, various issues
Note: LDC, less developed country.

Let us now consider the export shares of various countries in the Asian Pacific region. Table 2.10 reports that the proportion of US exports going to this part of the world increased from 13 per cent in 1960 to 28 per cent in 1990. The reason why there was no corresponding augmentation in the case of OECD Europe was entirely due to the spurt in intra-regional European trade.[7] In the 1980s, the Asian Pacific still accounted for a rapidly growing share of European exports, rising from 3.7 per cent in 1980 to 6.1 per cent in 1990. If European intra-regional trade is excluded, there is a marked increase in the share of European exports going to this region between 1960 and 1990 as well. For other developing countries, the Asian Pacific also absorbed a growing chunk of total exports. The exception is the formerly planned economies in Eastern Europe. Only 5 per cent of their total exports went to the Asian Pacific region in 1990.

The benefits of improved export opportunities due to larger

Table 2.10 Exports to the Asian Pacific region as a percentage of the total exports of each exporting country or country group, 1960–90

Country	1960	1970	1980	1990
United States	13.1	19.2	21.2	28.0
Canada	6.6	6.8	8.6	9.1
Europe (OECD)	5.8	4.6	3.7	6.1
Europe (OECD) (excl. intra-European trade)	13.4	13.6	11.4	29.4
Non-Asian Pacific LDCs (excl. China)	6.5	12.5	15.8	18.3
China	19.5	54.1	54.2	60.8
USSR, Eastern Europe	3.3	9.9	5.1	5.0

West European exports to Asian Pacific, by exporting country (per cent)

Country	Percentage	Country	Percentage
Germany	27.8	Denmark	2.3
Holland	4.8	Ireland	1.0
Italy	10.9	France	11.7
Greece	0.2	Portugal	0.3
Spain	1.8	UK	17.7
Belgium and Luxembourg	4.8		
Austria	1.7	Finland	1.4
Iceland	0.1	Norway	1.3
Sweden	4.0	Switzerland	8.2

Sources: See Table 2.9
Note: LDC, less developed country.

markets elsewhere usually do not need much argument to establish. However, a country exports basically to be able to pay for its imports. As long as it does not want to make donations to foreigners, or build up credits abroad purely for their own sake, this is the only reason to export. Hence, if newcomers on the world's economic scene provide opportunities for imports, this should be seen as an advantage.

Without doubt, consumers everywhere are quite willing to turn to goods provided by East Asian producers. Purchasers of capital goods and intermediate goods are similarly interested in buying from East Asia. According to Table 2.11, US imports from the Asian Pacific rose from some US$2 billion in 1960 to US$180 billion in 1990. Europe (OECD) imported just over US$3 billion in 1960, and US$140 billion in 1990. As a percentage of total imports, the United States imported 15 per cent from the Asian Pacific in 1960 and almost 35 per cent in 1990. During this period, the corresponding European (OECD) share rose from only some 6 per cent to 8.5 per cent.

The growth performance in East Asia has yielded advantages beyond the enlarged scope for trade. Competitive pressure has

Table 2.11 Principal countries and country groups importing from the Asian Pacific region, 1960–90 (billion US$)

Country	1960	1970	1980	1990
United States	2.3	9.7	66.1	181.1
Canada	0.2	0.9	4.6	15.1
Europe (OECD)	3.3	6.8	52.3	140.4
Non-Asian Pacific LDCs				
(excl. China)	1.9	4.6	42.6	54.4
China	0.1	0.8	7.6	28.9
USSR, Eastern Europe	0.4	0.9	7.6	6.9

Imports from Asian Pacific as a percentage of total imports of importing country

	1960	1970	1980	1990
United States	15.3	22.8	25.7	35.0
Canada	3.7	6.7	7.5	12.9
Europe (OECD)	5.8	4.6	5.8	8.5
Non-Asian Pacific LDCs				
(excl. China)	7.8	11.0	10.4	15.1
China	4.7	4.4	39.0	49.3
USSR, Eastern Europe	2.7	8.6	11.7	5.3

Sources: See Table 2.9
Note: LDC, less developed country.

increased in most industries, which should enhance the economic performance of all countries. Furthermore, there are new opportunities for investment nationally and internationally because of larger markets as well as a more rapid growth of technology. This has particularly been the case as Japanese investment in R&D has caught up and passed from copying to leading in a number of fields. The change has intensified the 'high tech' race; policy makers and executives in the United States and Europe are forced to try harder in order not to be outcompeted, and other countries are able to import new technologies.

The West has also learnt that investing in R&D and getting physical results is not enough. New knowledge must be put to productive use, and there are strikingly different performances in this respect. At the same time, it has become uncertain exactly what and how the West can learn from East Asia. There are varying feelings regarding whether joint projects and cooperation should be promoted, or whether new technology is something nations should try to keep to themselves. There are clearly options for gains from international technology transfers, and from various forms of collaborative efforts. On the other hand, it is obvious that valuable knowledge can be 'lost', and that a licensing arrangement can lead to unforeseen consequences in the hands of a creative imitator. Both the United States and the EC have consequently become ambivalent with respect to transfers of advanced technology. Investing in R&D themselves is increasingly important for the NIEs, although neither firms nor governments in developed countries have set out to coordinate any blockade in technology.

2.6 THE THREAT TO ESTABLISHED INTERESTS

East Asian competition, however, is not just experienced as a source of benefits. On the contrary, the producers exposed to it are seldom grateful. The United States as well as Europe have had much to say about the 'aggressive' behaviour of East Asian firms in Western markets. In addition, the Japanese in particular are accused of unfair collusion at home. Prices are kept high in Japan, and Japanese products are dumped in the West. As established interests are threatened in the West, there is considerable pressure for the adoption of countervailing duties, antidumping measures and 'voluntary' export restraints.

Such measures have contributed to the undertaking of substantial direct investment from East Asian countries within Western markets, most of it by Japanese firms. In many cases, this has created even fiercer competition for domestic industry. Again, there are loud accusations of unfair behaviour, predatory pricing, unholy corporate alliances to acquire Western technologies, lobbying to get favours, etc. In Europe, for example, Japanese direct investment has been named a 'Trojan horse'. Performance requirements, particularly local content rules which require that a certain share of parts and components are obtained locally, have been stipulated. In the eyes of some observers, the Japanese have been surprisingly willing to comply with demands for both voluntary export restraints and local requirements in foreign markets.

There are also complaints about the difficulties facing Western firms in East Asia, and particularly in Japan. 'Japan-bashing' has continued to increase in Washington during the last decade. The United States exerts considerable pressure on Japan not only to open its markets but also to increase its imports from the United States. The fact is, however, that Japan has reduced both its tariffs and its non-tariff barriers. Traditional trade obstacles – which are covered by GATT rules – are lower than, or as low as, in other industrial countries (International Monetary Fund 1988). In any case, they are certainly below those in the United States. Intensive criticism has continued against those import barriers which still exist – notably on agricultural products – and even more so against 'informal barriers', often referred to as 'structural impediments'.

Through the so-called 'Structural Impediments Initiative', the United States is trying to enforce various changes in Japanese society and the Japanese economy. Among other things, there are objections against the high costs and prices in Japan, long working hours, limited leisure time, high savings and excessively low consumption. Above all, Japan is asked to reform the multi-layer domestic distribution system, which prohibits or complicates the set-up of new shops as well as the introduction of new products.

There are diverse views on whether the Japanese market is 'closed' for foreigners. Leaving aside the favourite anecdotes and looking at some simple comparisons of import behaviour, it seems difficult to argue that Japan imports 'too little' from the United States. For example, while West Germany, France and Italy have a combined GDP which surpasses that of Japan, the

34

United States exported only US$31.2 billion to these countries in 1988, compared with US$37.7 billion to Japan.

Despite such observations, the fact remains that the Japanese market is tricky. While imports of industrial products in particular are extremely small, there is also limited activity by Western firms within the market. According to Encarnation (1992), US affiliates in the EC sold about six times the amount of US exports to the EC in 1989. In Japan, US affiliates were sold only about 1.5 times the amount of US exports. Thus, he argues, the key matter is not the failure of American-based firms to export to Japan, but rather the failure of US-owned firms to sell in Japan.

Criticism about protectionism has grown louder about the ANIEs as well, in parallel with their success in Western markets across the industrial spectrum. The fact is that they leave room for such accusations to a varying degree. Taiwan and especially Korea operate a number of import barriers, but less so than comparable developing countries. Export promotion also means that resources are not biased into import substitution. This makes the market mechanisms less distorted and, in effect, domestic markets less protected. Tariffs have been reduced and many other obstacles to imports have been dismantled during the last few years. Singapore is relatively open, and Hong Kong is the freest trader that exists. The developing countries in ASEAN, followers of the ANIEs in industrialization, are protected to a higher degree, especially the Philippines and Indonesia. However, even their trade policies are on average more liberal than those of other developing countries. The loud allegations on the part of many Westerners undoubtedly have a lot to do with the attempts to defend vested interests at home.

3

INTERNATIONALIZATION OF CORPORATE ACTIVITIES AND EAST ASIAN SOCIETIES

Trade in goods has in the last decades become closely related to industrial organization and foreign investment. Attention has been paid to imperfect competition, scale economies, imperfections in information and strategic behaviour, to mention a few factors which require considerable extensions of traditional economic models. Through direct investment in particular, so-called multinational firms are able to transfer technical and organizational abilities across national boundaries and specialize production internationally. This in turn affects the conditions for production and trade in various locations.

The overseas operations of multinational firms have also influenced the competition in production and trade between East Asia and Western economies. In particular, there is a sharp contrast between the success of Japanese firms across East Asia as well as within Western economies, and the difficulties that foreign firms have in succeeding in Japan.

Following a discussion of direct investment, and its relations with national economies, this chapter goes on to survey the special characteristics of Japan, and to some extent East Asia as a whole. With this foundation, the internationalization of business operations within East Asia, Japanese investment in the West and Western investment in Japan will be examined.

3.1 THE NATURE OF DIRECT INVESTMENT

Every economy has its special features which must be learned and handled by entrepreneurs, workers, consumers and citizens. Companies are typically domestic in character to begin with, as it is easiest to control and operate activities in the environment with which one is most familiar. Gradually, some firms set up subsidiaries abroad through direct investment, which involves an equity share in a foreign firm that is sufficiently large to establish lasting control. Such firms are here referred to as 'multinational'.[1]

In the early part of the twentieth century, direct investment was commonly undertaken in developing countries, and was widely viewed as a continuation of colonialism and exploitation. Lipson (1985) describes how the leading industrial powers, first Great Britain and later the United States, used overt or covert force to protect the interests of investors everywhere. In the late 1960s and early 1970s, however, the majority of developing countries undertook extensive nationalizations, i.e. seized equity with little or no compensation, without any significant retaliation from the home countries. The traditional rules had been dismantled.

The wave of nationalizations turned out to be a brief chapter in the history of direct investment. In the late 1970s, most countries ceased to nationalize, and during the 1980s the policy virtually disappeared. At the same time, taxes and performance requirements were lowered, and new efforts were made to attract investment. Key projects in natural resources had already been taken, falling commodity prices left firms with less profit to be captured by countries, and expanding financial markets provided nations with a stronger incentive to safeguard their reputation in economic transactions (Andersson 1991a). In addition, multinational companies adjusted and decomposed their production processes across countries. Activities in different economies became more integrated, leaving local governments with little to gain from further expropriation.

In the classic product-cycle theory, Vernon (1966, 1979) pointed out that new products are first developed in the industrial and technological centres of high-income countries. As long as there is a good deal of refinement and adjustment, and demand is fairly insensitive to price, production continues in this environment. When goods have matured, production is moved to medium-income countries. Later, when products and processing are standardized and competitiveness hinges primarily on labour costs, there is a relocation to the periphery of less developed countries.

Although Vernon's categorization still applies in many cases, multinationals are now based in each of the prime industrialized nations and have created complex networks of operations and transactions, principally in the advanced economies. By 1990, these countries accounted for some 75 per cent of the stock of direct investment. Investment in natural resources has become less prevalent, while manufacturing and finance have tended to predominate. Within the developing world, there has been a general reorientation of investment from countries that are heavily indebted and rationed in international capital markets, such as Latin America and Africa, to East and Southeast Asia (United Nations 1992).

At first, direct investment was evaluated on the same terms as portfolio investment, which is determined by inter-country differences in expected rates of return. Aliber (1970) saw the major motive as associated with capitalization on exchange risk, and the relative hardness of the home country's currency. Hymer (1960) was the first to observe that operations abroad are incompatible with perfect competition, since a firm suffers a handicap in a foreign market, for example with respect to information and knowledge of local conditions. For this reason, entry requires costs which are 'sunk' in a foreign market. The gap to neoclassical economics was narrowed by Kindleberger (1969) and Caves (1971), who connected direct investment to imperfections in goods and factor markets and economies of scale. Drawing on the insights about transaction costs provided by Coase (1937) and Williamson (1975), Buckley and Casson (1976) pointed out that internalization of activities within firms may be motivated by imperfections in information regarding technology, product quality or skills. The arguments have been synthesized in the eclectic or OLI framework (Dunning 1977), which is the basis for most current perceptions of direct investment. This framework stipulates three requirements for direct investment:

1 A firm must possess ownership-specific advantages, which may stem from access to inexpensive capital, a superior organization, distribution network, technology, facilities which enjoy economies of scale, or the ability to extract concessions from governments.
2 Internalization of such assets within the firm itself must be superior to trade at arm's length with other firms. Compared with licensing, for example, internalization may pay due to the secrecy and novelty of technology. On the other hand, riskiness in operations reduces the attractiveness of direct investment.
3 There must be locational advantages in internalization within a specific market. Country characteristics may be, for example, factor costs, geographical location in relation to markets for input or output goods, the quality of infrastructure, the size and

growth of the host country's market, taxes, regulations or other policies.

Direct investment may be motivated by the need of access to the host country's market. There may also be conditions or resources which are valuable because they, for instance, enhance the operations of a firm as a whole, or serve as a basis for exports either to third markets or back to the home country. There are at least three kinds of investment: first, horizontal enterprises with production abroad of the same line of goods; second, vertically integrated subsidiaries which transfer intermediate products; third, diversified affiliates which are neither horizontally nor vertically related to the rest of the organization. Some operations consist of coordination of activities rather than production in the traditional sense. Through any of these, firms reduce costs, obtain new information, adapt to the special demands of customers in foreign markets, tackle competitors and so on.

The way affiliates are established has gradually changed. The common entry mode used to be greenfield operations, i.e. subsidiaries were started 'from scratch'. Gradually, acquisition of already existing firms has become predominant. While this was initially used in industrialized countries, takeovers are now frequent almost everywhere. At first, this was viewed as a sign of greater instability and uncertainty in the world economy, as takeovers used to be less risky than greenfield operations but associated with lower expected rates of return (Caves 1982). Over time, however, greater organizational capacity and international experience have reduced the reliance of firms on their own technology. Firms are becoming more capable of adjusting already existing operations to their own objectives, as well as themselves benefiting from the skills of others.[3]

Apart from facilitating takeovers, these changes have opened up various opportunities for collaboration, in the form of joint ventures, licensing, turnkey contracts or other formal or informal (non-contractual) relations. Some studies emphasize the importance of informal information trading, which can be efficient because of low transaction costs. On the other hand, there is a lack of legal mechanisms to determine the distribution of rights and obligations (von Hippel 1987; Schrader 1991). In practice, formal and informal information trading often go together, and are influenced by management as well as the practices of researchers, engineers, marketing personnel and others.

The great costs that are required to develop modern technology, the risks of failure and the interest of firms in exploiting the technology of others while retaining their own, make the race for knowledge a key factor in international investment. Broadly speaking, the greater the speed with which know-how spills over to others, the smaller the return to the firm which generates it in the first place, while the potential for social benefits is greater. The pace with which technology is diffused depends on whether it is disembodied or embodied in, for example, products, processing, employees or other factors.

Although the data are scanty, we know that actual R&D typically represents only a fraction of the investment undertaken by firms to acquire industrial competence (Eliasson *et al.* 1990). Technology does not consist merely of generally applicable information, but there are attributes which are differentiated with respect to certain applications – and which interact with special production processes. The rapidly growing literature in this field has distinguished, for example, between knowledge that is universally available and that which is specific to firms.[2] The stages of *invention*, creating new ideas, and *innovation*, applying existing knowledge in product concepts, to some extent require different skills. It is well established that the handling of the two may involve trade-offs (Winter 1971; Levitt and March 1988).

The operations of a firm in a certain market will depend on whether it is able to transfer and apply its existing technology, expand it further or obtain new ones. Various factors will influence the outcome, of which some are associated with the firm itself, others with the host country (Kogut 1985; Porter 1986). Events in the home market, as well as the behaviour of other firms and countries, come into play as well. High labour intensity makes wages crucial, complex processes require access to engineers, large sunk costs call for economic and political stability, transport costs grow with geographical distance, pollutants make the environmental protection matter, etc. In addition, the location of firms and their mutual interactions shape the characteristics of economies.

3.2 INTERPLAY BETWEEN FIRMS AND COUNTRIES

The impact of direct investment on a host country can be contrasted with that of a financial flow. Instead of receiving a foreign firm, a country may borrow internationally and foster domestic firms. This means that the debtor country acquires immediate control over funds. If debt servicing becomes difficult, it finds itself constrained and subject to a repayment schedule that is unrelated to the state of its economy. With direct investment, on the other hand, the investing firm carries the risk of failure. That firm must expect to earn a risk premium if entering a market is to be attractive in the first place.

Although privileged financing does not generally constitute the crucial advantage that warrants direct investment, capital flows remain important. Multinational firms effectively channel liquidity across national boundaries, increasing the vulnerability of a country's external position. On the other hand, poor countries in particular may enjoy a financial stimulus as direct investment often goes along with foreign development assistance or portfolio investment. Even domestic savings, commonly argued to be discouraged by capital inflows, have been found to be favourably affected in East Asia (Gupta and Islam 1983; Lee et al. 1986). However, the contribution of capital is subordinate to the question of how the balance of payments is affected.

From the perspective of a host country, direct investment may stimulate exports and/or replace imports. On the other hand, foreign-owned subsidiaries tend to be more dependent on imported inputs than domestic firms are. For the home country, operations abroad may replace previous exports, but an expansion of sales also generates new exports of input goods or finished goods. The relationship between exports and direct investment is consequently uncertain, although most studies indicate a non-negative effect (Bergsten et al. 1978; Swedenborg 1979). As multinational firms enhance their international specialization, affiliates increasingly export to third markets or back to the home market. Although the home country thereby experiences a weakened trade balance, it may still benefit from the greater efficiency of industry.

Internationalization enables firms to exploit the special advantages offered by host countries. Their performance is very dependent on the degree to which they achieve this end. At the same time, locations are influenced by their activities through 'spin-off' effects. These occur through, for example, turnover of trained personnel, forward and backward linkages, and government officials. Firms are generally not able to appropriate all those rents which arise from their activities, resulting in externalities – effects that are not accounted for by those who are responsible for them (Pigou 1932).

Some external effects concern market structures. Moran (1985) reports contradictory influences on market concentration. Foreign investment may induce new competition and thereby stimulate efficiency in general. On the other hand, the sheer size of foreign-owned subsidiaries, their capacity to tackle bureaucracies, use of predatory pricing etc., may lead to the establishment of monopolies. The replacement of domestic monopolies by foreign monopolies is likely to be detrimental for a country, as profits are repatriated rather than reinvested. It is also possible that 'too poor' technologies are exported at 'too high' prices. In developing countries, domestic entrepreneurship may end up providing ancillary inputs (Lall and Streeten 1977).

However, the ultimate effects of direct investment on national economies hinge on the transfer of technology and skills in management, marketing, etc. Multinational firms are the major distributors of knowledge in both production processes and organization. They are also particularly efficient in realizing the potential of new technology and diffusing it internationally. Of the total international technology transfers, some three-quarters occur between OECD countries (Vickery 1986). A host country may receive know-how but a foreign firm may also engage in reverse technology transfers, i.e. absorb local ones and transfer them to other countries.

Although there is some variation between firms originating in different countries, multinational firms tend to retain some nine-tenths of their R&D at home.[4] The 'hard core' of R&D, the inventing stage, is typically located at the heart of large multi-national companies, but innovation evolves in various structures. Schumpeter (1939) stressed the importance of geographically concentrated clusters, in which skills are fostered among workers, within the educational system, and in networks of suppliers and distributors. Stiglitz (1987) spoke of localized learning effects. There is now a growing consensus in the literature about the importance of localized networks of economic and technological externalities. The quality and characteristics of the human work force plays an especially important role. Denison (1962) and Schultz (1963) have already highlighted the significance of investment in human capital. Azariadis and Drazen (1990) and Ljungqvist (1992) analysed the relationship between individuals' ability to accumulate human capital and economies' total stock of resources, demonstrating the prevalence of different possible states. The so-called endogenous growth literature, which aims at specifying how various assets determine the rate of technological progress and thereby influence the rate of growth, also explores this.[5]

With many firms making simultaneous location decisions, each influenced by others, there is an interdependence of behaviour. This makes it vital to consider 'systems' rather than bipolar relations between individual entities. For example, Wheeler and Mody (1992) found 'agglomeration economies' to be the main determinant of the location of US investment abroad. The 'optimal' amount of investment undertaken in a country by one firm increases the undertaking of investment by others.[6] There may then be multiple equilibria in investment, and in the quality of the factors of production which accompany it. Governments and exogenous factors also influence conditions through, for example, taxation, public transportation, the educational system and the legislative framework. An equilibrium may be more or less stable with respect to changing industry or country characteristics.

Apart from economic impacts, foreign firms may influence social, cultural, political or physical conditions in a host country. In his later work, Hymer was strongly critical of multinationals in this context. Walter (1972) predicted a relocation of pollution-intensive activities from rich to poor countries. As discussed in an 'unofficial' World Bank memo of January 1992, such relocation raises global welfare if pollution is located where it makes the least damage. Unfortunately, that outcome cannot be taken for granted. For example, autocratic regimes in particular may not act in the interest of social welfare, and environmental effects often transcend national boundaries.

Today, it has become better understood that monopolistic powers are increased by the prevention of entry by rival firms, rather than by the acceptance of foreign investment *per se*. With growing international experience, multinational firms tend not to clash or interfere with local customs, but play down their home country attributes in favour of local ones. Regarding the environment, it has been realized that multinational firms have a potential for developing and spreading cleaner and more effective technologies.

To sum up, the internationalization of business operations influences and transforms national economies. Direct investment involves transfers of capital, organization, management, technology, etc. These give rise to rents that individual firms cannot capture, but which affect other factors of production. The simultaneous location decisions of different firms are mutually interdependent. Together with externalities in, for example, knowledge and the fostering of human skills, this lays the basis for multiple equilibria. Activities based on advanced technology are particularly sensitive to appropriate infrastructure, the characteristics of the labour force and the proximity of other key activities.

3.3 CHARACTERISTICS OF JAPAN

While most of the literature on the internationalization of business operations has been concerned with multinational firms based in Western economies, the development in East Asia has given rise to new patterns. Before considering direct investment further, let us survey some special features of this part of the world. This section focuses on Japan, which still remains dominant in East Asia in economic terms. It discusses aspects of society which help to explain the growth performance of the region and which are of direct or indirect importance for corporate activities.

The nature of industrial organization is less well known in Japan than in other major developed countries, although it appears particularly important to understand. Over time, Japanese firms have shifted the basis of competitiveness with astonishing speed. Abegglen and Stalk (1985) mention stages in accordance with the following key factors: low wages, high-volume large-scale facilities, focused production and great flexibility. There are different views of which fundamental elements of Japanese organization enabled such swift and successful transformations, and the industrial advancement which has accompanied them.

As indicated by the circulation of daily papers given in Table 3.1, there is a generally high level of all-round education in Japan compared with other countries. In terms of formal education, Japan has the highest enrolment at the secondary level, and belongs to those with the largest share of graduates as well.[7] Concerning fields of specialization, there are relatively few undergraduate students in law and commerce, medicine and natural sciences, but many in engineering and social sciences.[8] The Japanese government spent some 17 per cent of total expenditure on education in 1987, which is less than the United States and only marginally more than most countries in Western Europe.

It is well established that Japanese students are trained in a

44

Table 3.1 Statistics on education

Countries	Percentage of age group with secondary level education	Estimated circulation of daily papers per capita	Graduates in 1989 (%) distributed by selected fields				
			Law and commerce	Engineering	Medical	Social science	Natural science
Japan	40	0.56	–	17	5	27	2
United States[a]	–	0.22	25	5	10	9	5
France[b]	–	0.19	26	6	10	7	14
West Germany[c]	18	0.34	8	17	24	13	5
Italy	11	0.10	14	7	26	15	7
The Netherlands[c]	9	0.31	13	6	12	16	4
Belgium[d]	13	0.22	22	6	14	12	7
UK[d]	–	0.42	27[e]	14	17	–	14
Sweden	36	0.53	11	29	23	2	2

Source: UNESCO 1991
Notes: [a] For 1985.
[b] For 1984.
[c] For 1988.
[d] For 1987.
[e] Figure for law only, as no information is given on commerce.

disciplinarian fashion up to university level, and show high basic skills by any international comparison. Once qualified for 'advanced studies', however, the emphasis lies on conceptual insights rather than technical capabilities or hard data. The crucial step is to get into the 'right' university, which channels graduates into the 'right' organization. The prestige of the university sends the main signal to the labour market, not the proven ability of the graduate. The educational system is actually subject to severe criticism, within Japan itself, for being outmoded. Several attempts at reform have been blocked by the political alliances built up over the years by the dominant LDP party (Schoppa 1991).

It is often claimed that the Ministry of International Trade and Industry (MITI) in particular, and the Ministry of Finance steer the direction of the Japanese economy. At the same time, a historical lack of authority is said to provide an incentive for the public sector to perform well in order to maintain its status. According to Johnson (1982), the Japanese government is 'developmentally-oriented', rather than 'regulatory-oriented'. The judicial system is small and conflicts are normally settled out of court through deals between the contenders themselves. The government interacts directly with firms in a coordinating function, which is both motivated and facilitated by the structure of social organization. Nakane (1970) pictured Japan as a 'frame' society with vertically organized groups subject to weak horizontal links. Through 'consensus formation', the government acts as a bridge-builder between competing private interests (Okimoto 1988).

The public sector has relied on incentives rather than command and, lacking legally enforceable means, it has been obliged to balance the use of threats, attractions and compromise. Domestic production of intermediate goods used to be protected, but there has still been fierce competition and exploitation of scale economies as the private sector has been required to accomplish international competitiveness. The policies pursued have contributed to an intricate network of inter-industry linkages, and improved the dissemination of information. Modern industries based on human skills and technology have benefited markedly from this development (Komiya 1975; Shinohara 1982).

Although MITI and other public institutions have played a major role in the past and still do so in many respects, their importance should not be exaggerated. Attention has now been paid to the internal organization of Japanese firms, and to inter-firm relations.

Dore's (1973) classic comparison between Japanese and British industry pictures Japan as an 'organization-oriented system', as differentiated from the 'market-oriented systems' of the West. Aoki (1988, 1990) has further distinguished between alternative modes of industrial organization on the basis of studies of American and Japanese firms.

Relatively speaking, Western firms thrive on specialized workers, and centralized information and decision-making. Orders are channelled hierarchically 'top-down', which accounts for many organizational layers and high costs for supervision and coordination. Japanese firms instead train workers extensively in various positions within a company through job rotation. There are often less strictly defined assignments, while workers are granted knowledge about product concepts as a whole. Strategic decisions are not imposed by top management on the basis of centralized information, but require consensus, and responsibilities are delegated to the operational level. Compared with Western firms, the Japanese adjust smoothly to small changes in demand, there is high wage flexibility and little unemployment.

Life-time employment, seniority wages and firm-specific unions are well-known generalizations of Japanese employer–worker conditions. To consider briefly some actual figures, let us compare the length of time that workers in Japan and a number of European countries remain with the same company. Table 3.2 reports the average number of years that male blue-collar and white-collar workers are employed. For Japan, a division is made for companies of different size. Firms are generally smaller in Japan than in other industrialized countries, and employment behaviour varies with the size of companies.

Except for the extremely service-oriented economy of Luxembourg, the length of employment is more extensive among white-collar than among blue-collar workers. Japan turns out not to have longer periods of service than most European countries. Although the average duration of employment is shortened by the large number of small firms, the same applies for blue-collar workers in large Japanese firms. For white-collar workers, there are fewer employees with short periods of service than in Western firms. This is particularly the case for large firms, which have a much greater share of workers employed for ten to nineteen years. For workers employed more than twenty years, there is not much of a difference even for the largest category of Japanese firms.

Table 3.2 Length of service for male workers in manufacturing, Japan and
the EC

Kind of workers	Country/company size	Years of service (%)			
		< 4	5–9	10–19	20–
Blue-collar workers	Japan/All companies	34.2	28.1	27.0	10.9
	/> 1,000 employees	23.3	29.9	31.3	15.5
	/100–999 employees	36.4	28.9	26.1	9.5
	/10–99 employees	43.6	25.5	23.0	7.8
	West Germany	45.6	17.1	24.5	12.8
	France	48.2	19.0	19.6	11.9
	Italy	46.0	22.0	21.9	8.9
	Belgium	46.4	19.6	20.1	13.9
	The Netherlands	45.7	18.7	21.2	14.5
	Luxembourg	32.3	17.2	27.0	23.5
	Great Britain	45.0	19.8	34.8	
White-collar workers	Japan/All companies	23.7	24.0	34.0	18.3
	/> 1,000 employees	15.6	22.0	37.7	24.7
	/100–999 employees	26.0	26.0	33.9	14.1
	/10–99 employees	36.9	25.1	26.8	11.3
	West Germany	34.5	17.6	27.4	20.5
	France	29.5	19.0	26.7	23.1
	Italy	39.8	21.0	26.2	12.1
	Belgium	31.8	19.8	24.4	24.0
	The Netherlands	31.0	18.0	27.3	23.6
	Luxembourg	28.8	21.9	27.4	21.8
	Great Britain	40.7	19.8	38.8	

Source: Koike 1988

The wage structure displays more clearcut differences. First, wages are less standardized in Japan than in Western countries. Work is priced within companies rather than in markets, which is in line with the prevalence of firm-specific unions. Second, there is a steeper wage profile in terms of age, applying both to blue-collar and white-collar workers, although it is more extreme for the latter. In 1989, Japanese male white-collar workers aged 50–4 earned some 250 per cent of what they did at the age of 21–4 (Ministry of Labour, various years). As of 1972, the ratio was 148 per cent in Western Germany for the same age group, 183 per cent in France and 195 per cent in Italy (European Community 1972).[9] For male blue-collar workers, the ratio was 175 per cent in Japan, compared with only 103 per cent in Germany and 110 per cent in France and Italy. The wage structure of blue-collar workers in Japan resembles that of white-collar workers in the West, which is associated with a 'white-collarization' at the shop floor. For both categories, promotion is slow and employers retain salary increases until 'old age', keeping them as a 'hostage' which induces hard work. Again, there are exceptions. Female employees in Japan do not follow the same pattern, as they are not generally expected to pursue a lasting working career.

However, there is a marked tendency in Japan to train and keep key employees. Graduates from the most prestigious universities, for example, normally stay with the same employer through most of their career. On the whole, remuneration and promotion encourage 'committed' employer–worker relations, which facilitate learning, cooperation, reliability, etc.[10] Compared with Western economies, one can observe considerably longer working hours in Japan. The official statistics may well underestimate the difference, since it does not include unpaid overtime work, which is known to be extensive in small Japanese companies. Long working hours and limited leisure time in turn contribute to high savings for the future, rather than consumption. International comparisons of labour productivity are not very informative, however, because of the sensitivity to exchange rates and real prices.[11]

As seen from a questionnaire directed to 700 companies, there are notable differences in employment behaviour even between Japanese-owned and foreign-owned firms in Japan. The former value a long career within the company more highly in terms of promotion, train a greater proportion of their staff from graduation onwards, allow for fewer of those newly employed to start work without specific training in the company, and use firing less often as a means to lay off workers (Odaka 1990).

The conditions in the labour market reflect the characteristics of the Japanese economy and society as a whole. It is often argued that Japan exhibits 'high trust' between fellow citizens. Arrow (1969, 1974) viewed trust as a public good which facilitates the exchange of information and the development of new technologies, and which may differ between cultures. Others have considered trust as a psychological condition which has a bearing on the personality characteristics of individuals (Deutsch 1958). Luhmann (1979) emphasized the role of trust in reducing uncertainty about the future. It remains unclear how trust between individuals relates to external conditions, however. Postponing further discussion on the source and nature of 'trust', we can observe that the Japanese economy in many ways benefits from communication and exchange of information between counterparts who form long-standing relationships on the basis of implicit contracts.

In Japan, there is generally a limited need to internalize activities in a company. Hostile takeovers, through which corporate control is traded in Western economies, are uncommon in Japan. Rather than being owned by shareholders, firms 'belong to' all those interests which are tied to them for the long term: banks, workers, suppliers, creditors, clients, etc. Companies disconnect activities which are not crucial to their organization, accounting for relatively small firms on average. Small size facilitates the sharing of information and responsibilities within firms. 'Core' firms and suppliers develop a high degree of complementarity without formal control. This enhances skills which are tailored to the specific counterpart, contributing a more rapid introduction of new technologies and fewer defective products than in corresponding Western relations (Asanuma 1988, 1989; Clark *et al.* 1987).

'Main banks' serve as the core of industrial groups, *keiretsu*, in which firms are tied together by cross-owning of equity, as well as by various formal and informal links. These banks finance long-term projects, assist in the dissemination of information and act as lenders of last resort in times of crisis. In such groups, behaviour has been found to be less marked by liquidity constraints than in other firms in Japan (Hoshi *et al.* 1991). Jenson (1989) points out that the regulatory system enables financial institutions to be 'active investors'. The large shareholders in *keiretsus* tend also to be major debt-holders, and have a range of other relations with firms. Hence, management is subject to a considerable influence through various channels (Kester 1990). In times of distress or failure, main banks may intervene and replace the management. Such links substitute for an external takeover and bankruptcy mechanism. Compared with the United States, there is generally more direct monitoring of executives in Japan (Sheard 1991; Prowse 1992).

Within the corporate networks, there is above all an intense process of learning through continuous interactions between users and producers, including researchers, manufacturers, marketing personnel, etc. While Japan still plays a fairly small role in terms of 'patented' technology, progress emanates from an accumulation of minor improvements in product development, automation, quality standards and rationalization. Innovations emerge from the 'overlapping' of different stages of operations, and from an extensive sharing of information (Imai 1990). The interplay in electrical engineering between departments that specialize in R&D and operative departments is one typical example (Wakasugi 1991). This set-up contrasts with the traditional Western image of a linear development from invention through prototypes to mass production. While cooperating in R&D, however, Japanese firms compete fiercely in goods markets. Recalling the distinction between different kinds of knowledge, the Japanese cooperate effectively among each other to enhance generally useful technology, while at the same time competing in exploiting it with the help of specific capabilities.

Explanations of the ability to engage in continuous relations in Japan often point to the country's special culture and history, and particularly the 250 years of isolation during the Tokugawa period. As is well known, cooperative behaviour is supported when transactions are repeated many times (Axelrod 1984). The traditionally feudal Japanese society and low mobility has laid the basis for strong reputation effects. This applies to individuals as well as families or groups of various kinds, accounting for a sincere desire not to damage the reputation of other members. Psychiatrists stress the motivation to acquire social 'harmony' and particularly a sense of belonging – reflected in the concept *amae* – which is traced to close ties between mothers and children (Takeo 1973).

On the other hand, many of the characteristics of modern Japan evolved only in the 1950s or even 1960s. Dore (1973) and Koike (1984) observed differences in production technology that emanated from the relatively late industrialization, especially at the new start after the Second World War. It is possible that Europe, which industrialized first, got the most developed external markets. When Japan industrialized, appropriate organizational structures had already been created, which may have contributed to weaker external markets. Ito (1989) emphasized the interplay between social and economic factors. The high growth in Japan in the postwar period made it important to focus on the expansion of capacity rather than short-term profitability. At the same time, the historically and socially determined presence of strong reputation effects favoured loyalty and commitment in business relations as a means of expansion.

51

The differences between Japan and other countries should not be overstated. Main-bank arrangements are far from universal in Japan, and cross-owning of shares exists in the West as well. The point is that the Japanese economy as a whole forms a special set-up. Investment in workers' skills and underpaid wages in the early stages of a career would not be possible if practised only by certain firms. Similar conditions support the structure of the financial market, and the absence of a visible market for 'corporate control'. External markets are relatively undeveloped, but there are effective mechanisms within and between organizations to steadily upgrade the crucial linkages. Thus, the Japanese economy can be interpreted as a special 'equilibrium', which is separate from that, or those, prevailing in Western countries. Actors behave in a certain way because 'the others' do too (Kanemoto and MacLeod 1989; Andersson, 1992b; Okuno-Fujiwara 1993). Friedman and Fung (1992) model this in terms of an evolutionary game. In Japan, firms are more capable of upgrading the skills of employees than in Western economies, because workers do not have as many opportunities to make use of them elsewhere. Although the Japanese economy is then more effective, it would not be sustainable in the event that the two systems were mixed and labour mobility increased.

The Japanese are at present battling with the normalization of equity prices, which have been even more inflated in Japan than in other countries.[12] Some predict that the rise of Japan is a temporary rather than a permanent phenomenon. Growth has slowed and funds are brought back home to support faltering accounts. While Japanese consumption has fallen, however, exports and the trade surplus keep growing. Here, we have focused on the special features of Japan rather than evaluated current and future issues. These will be returned to in subsequent chapters.

3.4 HUMAN AND SOCIAL ASPECTS IN EAST ASIA

The countries in East Asia display certain similarities. The most advanced economies are all conspicuously devoid of natural resources. An effective management of labour and corporate relations is the fundamental cornerstone of development. At the same time, each country is characterized by specific conditions. Since the Korean home market is much smaller than Japan's, it has been less feasible to stimulate competition behind protectionist barriers. There have consequently been weaker inter-industry linkages, and less of a feedback relationship between exports and domestic demand. The government has supported the growth of already large firms rather than new ones (Song 1990). The other ANIEs are even smaller, and there has not been a basis for any meaningful import substitution policy in any of them, although Singapore tried for a few years in the 1960s when it formed a union together with Malaysia.

Throughout East Asia, rapid growth has been associated with an expansion of labour input in manufacturing. In the 1950s and 1960s, all the ANIEs had extensive underemployment, which is a more applicable concept than unemployment in economies without well-developed welfare systems, and a rapid population increase. In the 1980s and 1990s, there has instead been full employment, and even a labour shortage. There were about four times more jobs in manufacturing in Korea and Taiwan by 1988 than there had been two decades earlier (Galenson 1992). Malaysia and Thailand have achieved almost as impressive growth rates, although at a lower level. Their agricultural sectors have also absorbed more of the work force, at least seasonally. The notable exception is the Philippines, where the level of underemployment has been estimated to be as high as 30 per cent (Economic Development Authority 1984).

Apart from the absorption of underemployed labour, the manufacturing sectors of the ANIEs and ASEAN have achieved a remarkable increase in productivity compared with other developing countries. The growth of real output per employee in manufacturing is shown in Table 3.3. Once again, the Philippines constitutes an exception. Labour productivity more than doubled in Korea between 1970 and 1980. Between 1980 and 1986, it increased by an additional 59 per cent, compared with 40 per cent in Thailand and 26 per cent in Taiwan. This improvement in labour productivity, in parallel with the expansion of employment, implies an extremely high level of savings and investment efficiency.

It has been noted that governments play an active role in East Asia. Acceptable infrastructure has been provided, a sound macro-economy has been safeguarded, and substantial resources have been allocated to education and training. In addition, the promotion of certain strategic industries has given rise to technological spillovers

Table 3.3 Development of real output in manufacturing per employee
(1980 = 100)

Year	South Korea	Malaysia	Philippines	Taiwan	Thailand
1970	40	96	102	62	70
1975	71	94	125	72	76
1980	100	100	100	100	100
1985	140	136	105	118	138
1986	160	–	111	126	140

Source: World Bank 1989–90; Republic of China 1989

and various linkages to domestic industry. To name one example, the steel company Pohang Iron and Steel (Posco) has influenced the industrialization process in South Korea, and beyond, by providing a range of industries with first class steel at competitive prices.

Like other related projects, Posco was supported in order to generate dynamic efficiency gains across a wide industrial spectrum, rather than to create jobs. The links between public planners and the private sector have not merely served to steer or guide the latter, or to provide compensation and privilege. The private sector has carried the major responsibility for development and has been expected to achieve results. The most authoritarian leadership has been exerted in Korea, where there is less emphasis on social harmony than in Japan, and greater appreciation of individualistic forces. As in the rest of East Asia, however, there is a considerable Confucian influence, and organization is based on the principles of the family. The virtues of loyalty and integrity appear to be as pronounced in Korea as in Japan, although they are relatively more one-sided and less reciprocal, which accounts for minor frictions in cooperation and information sharing.

In the other successful economies in the region, Chinese emigrants play a major role. The overseas Chinese are well known for their entrepreneurial spirit and networks of business contacts. Firms are based on family control and capital accumulation. They remain small and are run in an autocratic manner. At the same time, there is intense exchange and cooperation between firms. In China itself, the last decade has seen an extremely rapid growth of rural enterprises. Between 1978 and 1990, they expanded from 28 to 93 million employees, absorbing (at least on a part time basis) 22 per cent of the rural labour force. Their share of national output increased from 7 per cent to 25 per cent over this period (*Zhongguo Xiangzhe Qiye Bao* 1992). The characteristics of these firms are a reflection of Chinese agrarian society. As among overseas Chinese, there is a web of kinship between firms, as well as between firms and local authorities.

On the whole, growth has taken place in a framework that combines human learning, initiative and openness with political, social and economic stability. This is obvious in China, where growth began with the reforms of the late 1970s. When the situation was shaken in 1989, production stagnated. In the first nine months of 1992, when stability as well as openness was restored, national income grew by 12 per cent on an annual basis. Industrial output rose by almost 30 per cent compared with the year before.

Korea and Taiwan had, like Japan, extensive land reforms after the Second World War.[13] As noted by Adelman (1977), there were also sweeping educational reforms prior to the takeoff in growth. These policies contributed to a relatively equal wealth and income distribution and the evolvement of highly capable labour forces. In fact, East Asia contradicts the view of a conflict between development and equity, laid out by Kuznets (1965). Korea did experience growing income differences in its early industrialization, but that phase was quickly concluded. In Taiwan, which has the most advanced social security system of the ANIEs, higher growth and increased equity have accompanied each other. The notable exception is, once again, the Philippines. Like most Latin American countries, it has been trapped for decades in a spiral of social instability and corruption.

It is true that Thailand, Malaysia and Indonesia also have large disparities in income distribution. However, the ownership of land is more dispersed in these countries compared with the Philippines, which accounts for fairly stable rural conditions. In Malaysia, the desire to upgrade the economic position of the poorer Malay majority relative to the Chinese minority led to a redistribution of ownership and incomes under the New Economic Policy (1971–90). The effects were questionable, since new gaps and injustices emerged instead of the old ones. All three countries have problems with vested interests that benefit from protectionist measures. Nevertheless, industrialization has been largely devoted to the exploitation of comparative advantage, and there has been a more effective use of the labour force than in the Philippines.

Broadly speaking, East Asia has embarked on industrialization in societies with stable and equitable conditions. Governments have provided infrastructure and supported strategic investments. The accomplishment of international competitiveness has been the over-shadowing objective. Development has first and foremost been achieved through good management of labour and the fostering of rewarding human relations. This applies to East Asia as a whole, although there are many sharp differences between the individual societies and economies. The internationalization of business operations within the region should be seen against this background.

3.5 THE FLYING WILD GEESE

In terms of level of development, factor endowments and natural resources, East Asia contains a range of dissimilar economies. At the one extreme is Japan, with a skilled and fully employed labour force, high wages, financial resources and modern technology, but with hardly any natural resources. The ANIEs largely resemble Japan in these respects, but wages are lower and technologies better suited to the exploitation of cheap labour. Countries like Malaysia and Indonesia are rich in natural resources, but have insufficient capital and modern technology. In the neighbouring countries of China and Vietnam, there are large inexpensive and underemployed labour forces. The differing conditions account for complementarity between the economies in the region.

Meanwhile, differences in culture and management style impede the establishment of mutual understanding. Chen (1992), for example, reports frictions with Japanese investors in China due to variation in values. To this can be added the animosities that prevail between peoples in the region, including those that remain from the military expansion of the Japanese in the first part of the twentieth century. Despite the difficulties, there has been an extensive economic integration through investment.

Although South Korea borrowed heavily in the late 1970s, and the Philippines, Malaysia and Indonesia have troublesome debts, there has generally been less portfolio investment than in most other developing countries. Official assistance from the United States contributed to setting off growth in Japan, South Korea, Taiwan and Indonesia, but the amount has not been exceptional. Compared with other developing regions, only direct investment has reached notable proportions in East Asia.

The links between public and private capital should not be underestimated. In the case of Japan, official development assistance and private investment have mainly targeted the same countries.

The bulk of aid has been connected with Japanese business activities, although the tied share is reported to have declined in recent years. Official development assistance has provided strategically important investment in infrastructure, which the recipient countries would hardly have been able to afford on their own. In addition, the Japanese government has actively assisted its private industry with the provision of information on country characteristics, suitable local partners, availability of skilled workers, etc.[14]

Direct investment has played a major role in East Asia for a long time. In the wake of colonization there was substantial European investment in extraction and distribution of natural resources, especially in Singapore, Malaysia and Indonesia. The United States subsequently became the predominant source of direct investment, focusing on the Philippines and Taiwan in addition to the countries just mentioned. Driven by its desire to acquire secure access to raw materials, Japanese companies were also active in Southeast Asia at an early stage.

By 1979, Japanese direct investment could match that of the United States, and had certainly surpassed that from Europe, in most of East and Southeast Asia. However, satisfactory data from the same source are not available on total and Japanese flows.[15] The broad pattern should still be apparent, with a strong Japanese presence in Singapore, Indonesia and Hong Kong relative to the size of the host economy. Compared with the total flow of direct investment, Japanese firms were particularly active in Thailand, Indonesia and Korea. In South Asia, on the other hand, there was no Japanese direct investment at all. The situation was the same in China, which was virtually closed up to that time.

What is more noteworthy in Table 3.4 is the increase in the size of Japanese direct investment in the 1980s relative to the size of the host economies. While some attractions in the region have already been indicated, developments in Japan itself, as well as in the West, have played a significant role as well. Financial deregulation and integration, following the overhaul of Japan's foreign exchange law in 1980, enabled the financial institutions to expand worldwide. The rising yen and higher costs for labour, land and inputs in general made it expensive to produce at home. That the ANIEs and ASEAN had their currencies more or less pegged to the dollar

Table 3.4 Stocks of total and Japanese direct investment in Asian countries

Host countries	Total direct investment Stock as a percentage of GDP 1979	Japanese direct investment Stock as a percentage of GDP 1979	Stock as a percentage of GDP 1989	Percentage increase in Japanese direct investment over GDP 1979–89
East Asia				
ANIEs				
Korea	2.8	1.8	2.1	17
Taiwan	n.a.	0.8	1.8	125
Singapore	24.9	7.6	22.2	192
Hong Kong	11.1	4.2	17.3	312
ASEAN				
Malaysia	17.0	2.4	6.7	179
Thailand	1.7	1.2	5.1	325
Philippines	6.0	1.6	3.2	100
Indonesia	8.3	5.4	11.8	119
China	0.0	0.0	0.6	–
South Asia				
Bangladesh	0.1	0.0	0.0	0
India	1.9	0.0	0.0	0
Pakistan	3.8	0.0	0.0	0
Sri Lanka	3.1	0.0	0.0	0

Sources: Calculations on the basis of World Bank, *World Development Report*, various issues; Asian Development Bank 1990; UNCTC 1983; Ministry of Finance 1991

further contributed to making production there competitive. Barriers to imports in the West motivated production either within those markets themselves or in third countries from which exports could be shipped.

Meanwhile, the information provided by public institutions as well as by their private partners has facilitated investment abroad especially for small and medium sized Japanese firms. As small firms typically have a limited ability to collect information about foreign markets, Japan displays a unique record in this respect. In 1989, 54 per cent of all cases of Japanese direct investment was undertaken by small and medium sized firms. Some 65 per cent were located in Asia. Their single most important motivation was reported to be the 'need of reducing labour costs', which were burdensome because of the rising yen. Increasing exports back to Japan have been recorded from small Japanese firms in recent years (Ministry of International Trade and Industry 1992).

Between 1979 and 1989, the stock of Japanese direct investment relative to GDP at least doubled in three of the ANIEs and in ASEAN. The largest expansion took place in Thailand, Hong Kong, Singapore and Malaysia. Within the region, the absolute increase in the flow was larger, the lower the income level of the host country, the lower the tax and the more sizeable and open the host country. The absolute increase was larger in sectors based on low technology and skill intensity, but the relative increase was greater in advanced sectors (Andersson and Burenstam Linder 1991). The South Asian countries still did not obtain any investment, partly because of restrictions on trade and inward investment.

Japanese researchers have argued for a special 'Japanese' product life cycle, in which Western technologies are adjusted to suit conditions in developing countries (Kojima 1973; Ozawa 1979). By exploiting locational advantages throughout East Asia, Japanese firms cut costs and expand industries which are in line with the special advantages of each country. As incomes and wages have grown, however, the Japanese firms have upgraded the capital and skill intensity of their operations in the ANIEs and ASEAN, and located labour-intensive activities in poorer countries.

In the last decade, the Japanese firms have met fierce competition from Taiwan, Hong Kong and Singapore. These have taken over a great deal of the previously 'Japanese' role in export-oriented labour-intensive manufacturing. Taiwan and Hong Kong have established the largest operations in Southeast Asia as a whole, while Singapore has invested primarily in Malaysia. Thailand obtained about half of the total intra-Asian direct investment between 1986 and 1989, while Indonesia and Malaysia were the second most important destinations. Hong Kong and Taiwan, the latter through Hong Kong, were the main investors in China, where they provided an estimated two-thirds of the total flow of direct investment between 1978 and 1988 (Asian Development Bank 1991).

The internationalization of business operations is far from the only factor behind growth in East Asia. Japan itself, like Korea, used to adopt a restrictive attitude towards foreign investment. Favourable economic, political and social conditions set the stage for development in the first place, and for the attraction of direct investment in the second. Given the right conditions and access to information, however, private firms have been able to take on entrepreneurial risks. In this capacity, they have transferred appropriate technologies and stepped up the division of labour. Balassa (1991) emphasizes the impact that foreign investment has had on efficiency, incomes and savings in East Asia, while Naya (1990) underscores the positive effects on exports.

In the late 1980s, there was a substantial spurt in intra-Asian trade. Intra-Asian exports grew at 23 per cent per annum over 1986–9. This did not emanate from Southeast Asia, although ASEAN granted trade preferences. Rather, Japan and the ANIEs accounted for almost 70 per cent of the intra-Asian exports as of 1989. Today, some 70 per cent of all regional trade consists of manufactured products, with petroleum from Indonesia and Malaysia representing the only primary products of significance. Trade among the ANIEs is also important, mainly because of Hong Kong's role as an *entrepôt* for exports from China. The flows of direct investment within East Asia have speeded up the specialization of production in this part of the world. The 'Flying Wild Geese' is a popular metaphor for the development process resulting from the mobility and flexibility of private business in the region. Following the 'leading goose' in a wide formation, the individual countries move up the industrial ladder one after the other, chasing those ahead as changes in factor price relations alter their comparative advantages (Shinohara 1972).

Thus, private firms have been able to take on entrepreneurial risks across East Asia. Satisfactory infrastructure, a loyal and ambitious working force and stable conditions account for a profitable playing field. Corporate activities have utilized favourable conditions for close and lasting networks within as well as between firms, although the way of management varies between the different countries. These have contributed both to international specialization of production and to the diffusion of technologies. There is little fear that Japan, or the other home countries, would become 'deindustrialized' as a consequence. Crucial, advanced activities do not leave their home base. By expanding operations throughout the region, East Asian firms have acquired the strength and experience to proceed further, this time to Western economies. Firms from the ANIEs are following the Japanese in this respect as well.

3.6 JAPANESE FIRMS IN THE WEST

For a long time, the special features of the Japanese economy and society were believed to be incompatible with successful operations in Western countries on any large scale. With Western worker mobility and attitudes towards unions, wages, financing, owner-ship, etc., Japanese firms were not believed to be competitive. In the 1970s, however, the Japanese became conspicuously successful in the West in certain business sectors. Financial institutions had already entered at an earlier stage. Coulbeck (1984) described how they originally came to the West to support a limited amount of direct investment abroad by their domestic industrial partners. With the expansion of the Eurodollar markets, a new era began.

Low capital standards and dividend pressure made it possible for Japanese financial institutions to focus on size and market share. Thereby, they were in a position to take advantage of the large supplies of capital which emanated from the savings surplus of the OPEC countries after the oil price rises. In the 1980s, they could invest in US securities, while their financial markets at home were slowly liberalized. Further supported by high savings at home, the current account surplus and the appreciation of the yen from 1985, there has been a rapid growth in the total international assets of Japanese banks. While they still lagged behind US banks in 1983, they grew to more than three times their size in 1990. The increase largely consisted in short-term borrowing and long-term lending, which indicates that the Japanese assimilated international risks.

The Japanese advancement in trade and portfolio investment was at first unmatched in direct investment. Until the late 1970s, it comprised only about 1 per cent of total fixed capital formation,

61

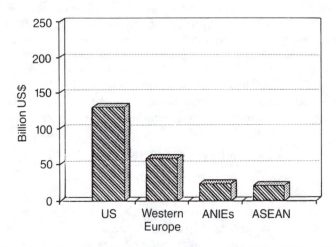

Figure 3.1 Stocks of Japanese direct investment in 1990 (billion US$)
Source: Ministry of Finance 1991

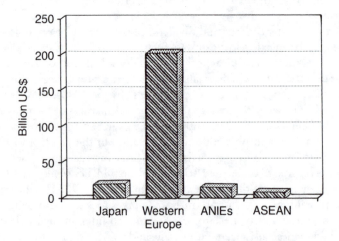

Figure 3.2 Stocks of US direct investment in 1990 (billion US$)
Source: Department of Commerce 1992

compared with 3 per cent in Germany or 4.5 per cent in the United States. In the late 1980s the situation changed. Figures 3.1 and 3.2 show the stock of Japanese and US direct investment in the most important regions as of 1990. In spite of the difficulty in comparing data from different countries, it is still worth noting that the American firms were ahead only in Western Europe (not considering other regions, such as Latin America). Parallel to its expansion in the 1980s, the Japanese direct investment became much more disposed geographically. The share accounted for by Asian countries was halved from 28 per cent in 1983 to 14 per cent in 1989.

The United States has taken over as the dominant location for Japanese direct investment, but the stock of investment in Western Europe has also exceeded that in Asia. The service industry is relatively more important in the United States and Europe, accounting for about 70 per cent of the total stock in these regions. Asia remains of great importance in manufacturing, where it has continued to attract almost the same amount of Japanese direct investment as Europe, while the United States still remains far ahead.

It is sometimes argued that the spurt in Japanese direct investment was guided by MITI, in order to steer off the call for protection in Western markets. The truth is, however, that it was unavoidable once Japan liberalized its foreign exchange laws. Most fundamentally, technological progress in communication, information processing, financial systems and transportation allowed firms to expand their organizational and managerial capabilities generally. The increasing complexity of products has also made it necessary to be present in foreign markets in order to adapt to the special priorities of customers, and in order to learn from others. As Japanese firms used to lag behind, the changing circumstances forced an expansion of operations in the West in order to catch up.

In the United States, the overvalued dollar might have been expected to discourage direct investment in the early 1980s. On the other hand, the high level of consumption provided a strong 'pull' factor. The twin deficits tapped the United States of financial resources, and made American firms price-worthy and easily accessible in spite of the high dollar. In addition, direct investment by the Japanese in the United States, as in the UK, fostered valuable management skills in banking and securities, where Japan has been subject to domestic regulations. They were also able to acquire Western production technologies, not least through the acquisition of strategically important US firms. Capital participation in joint projects is also a common means of entry into the United States.

The Japanese have been able to adjust their management in order to operate successfully within Western markets. Crucial activities in R&D remain concentrated at home, however. As discussed above, innovations emanate from the overlapping system and information sharing which is tailored to the special conditions within Japan.[16] At the same time, the Japanese have been able to bring along some of their links from home, such as those connected to financial institutions and suppliers. They have also applied part of their domestic management practices overseas. Top managers are almost always of Japanese nationality, while blue-collar workers tend to be successfully adapted to job rotation and 'on the job training'. The observed result has been higher motivation on the shop floor, e.g. in Great Britain. White-collar workers, on the other hand, have been less satisfied, leading to a higher turnover of personnel (Trevor 1989; Yasui *et al.* 1989).

There have been many complaints by the Japanese concerning conditions in Western economies, such as the emphasis on individual efforts and a generally weak group orientation. In some respects, the Japanese have effectively adjusted their behaviour to local practices. For example, they frequently apply takeovers to gain access to technologies, brand names, distribution networks, etc., which is in sharp contrast to the customs in Japan. Joint ventures are also becoming common, workers are employed in mid-career to a higher degree than in Japan, etc.

In the late 1980s, the growing Japanese presence turned into a source of political friction in the United States. The downturn of the US economy together with favourable prospects in the Single Market, made Europe a more viable alternative destination. The investment by Japanese firms between 1986 and 1989 was equivalent to two-thirds of their total investment in the EC between 1951 and 1989. Similar to its increased geographical dispersion within the United States, Japanese investment has also become much more diversified in terms of location in different European countries. According to Encarnation (1992), Japanese firms sold three times the exports from home in both the United States and the EC in 1989.

There are notable differences between Japanese direct investment in the United States and in the EC, however. For example, affiliates in Europe are normally owned by parent companies which are present in the United States as well, while the opposite may not hold. The large networks of Japanese affiliates in the United States in the supply of motor vehicle parts and electronic parts have not yet been established in Europe. Acquisitions of local firms are more common in the United States, where Japanese firms are more prepared to diversify into local industries. In Europe, this has mainly occurred in non-electrical machinery.

As in the United States, a range of factors specific to the EC have made it an attractive location. As they used to lag behind in Europe more than elsewhere, the strive for globalization motivated a particularly great expansion by Japanese direct investment in this part of the world. The prospects of one large market also spurred direct investment as a complement to exports in the late 1980s. The risk of increased protectionism – a 'Fortress Europe' – played a role in this respect. On the other hand, there seem to have been fewer attractions in the form of access to local technology. We return to these matters in Chapter 5.

3.7 WESTERN FIRMS IN JAPAN

The undertaking of direct investment in Western markets has not eliminated Japan's trade surplus. This should come as no surprise when judged against standard economic indicators, such as terms of trade changes or savings behaviour. However, the limited size of manufactured imports and inward investments in particular cannot be explained in sanguine terms (Krugman 1987; Saxonhouse and Stern 1989). Although there is a high price level in Japan overall, Western goods tend to be even more expensive than the average. Still, Japanese consumers have been found mostly to respond normally to changing prices (Lawrence 1987).[17] The absence of any major formal barriers to trade would seem to suggest some invisible barrier to entry, which causes a mark-up on the price of Western products in Japan.

The limited supply and high prices could be expected to attract direct investment for the purpose of providing foreign products more effectively. It is sometimes argued that only a short period of time has elapsed since the liberalization started in the early 1980s, and that imports and inward investments have picked up quickly since then. In the case of inward direct investment, there was an increase from about US$0.8 billion on average in 1982–4, to US$3 billion in 1988–9. Nevertheless, the size of the Japanese economy, and the time which has passed, should account for an even greater difference. The inflow has in any case been dwarfed in relation to the outflow.

Table 3.5 reports inflows and outflows of direct investment between 1981 and 1990 for OECD countries. The first column shows the outflow in billion US dollars, the second the inflow and the third the ratio between the inflow and the outflow. What separates Japan from other countries is the extreme imbalance. According to Japanese Ministry of Finance data, the stock of American direct investment in Japan was 7 per cent of the stock of Japanese direct investment in the United States in 1989. The direct investment from the EC in Japan was 6 per cent of the Japanese direct investment in the EC.

Many Western firms are, of course, highly successful in Japan. The Ministry of International Trade and Industry (1991) reports, for example, that foreign firms are above average in profitability. On the basis of data from 520 foreign firms in Japan, JETRO (1990a) stresses the importance of the brand name, technology or

Table 3.5 Cumulative flows of direct investment, OECD countries 1981–90

Country	Outward direct investment (in billion US$)	Inward direct investment (in billion US$)	Inward relative to outward direct investment
United Kingdom	188	122	0.65
West Germany[1]	86	18	0.21
France[1]	86	43	0.50
Italy[1]	28	25	0.89
The Netherlands	52	28	0.54
Belgium and Luxembourg	21	28	1.33
Spain	8	46	5.75
Finland	12	3	0.25
Norway[1]	9	5	0.56
Sweden	45	8	0.18
Austria	4	3	0.75
Switzerland	32	12	0.38
United States	174	366	2.10
Canada	37	11	0.30
Japan[1]	186	3	0.02
Australia	23	39	1.70

Source: OECD/DAF – based on official national statistics from the balance of payments converted in dollars at daily average exchange rate
Note: [1] Reinvested earnings are not included in national statistics.

concept uniqueness. A unique product, high quality and after-sales service are keys to success. Provided that they manage to establish themselves, foreign firms often achieve handsome profits in Japan.

However, the initial stage of operations in Japan tends to be long and costly. Aquisitions of already established firms, which has become the dominant entry mode in other markets, is hampered by the local conditions (Andersson 1992c). In addition, the major problems are associated with the ability of local competitors to catch up in technology and the establishment of functioning relations with locals – including the hiring of qualified local staff. Licensing contracts often turn out as disappointments, because time runs out or products are copied. Hedlund (1993) observes connections between the complexity of the distribution networks adopted by Swedish firms in Japan and the ability of local competitors to catch up in technology. Substantial obstacles are also reported in dealings with local agents and government authorities. The same Japanese who flexibly adjust in relation to each other as well as in operations abroad appear quite inflexible *vis-à-vis* foreigners in the Japanese market.

What is the source of the alleged difficulties for Westerners in their interactions with locals in Japan? Let us review some possible explanations. The 'overlapping' system, through which information is channelled back and forth between research, production and marketing, has been argued to put foreigners at a disadvantage. Partnerships with Westerners, who do not apply such overlapping, would be asymmetric since knowledge diffuses faster on the Japanese side. The Western side finds that Japanese partners do not adhere to their alliances, and mutual trust is difficult to establish (Hamel *et al.* 1986).

As mentioned above, Westerners tend to invest and pursue efforts which make them efficient in external markets, i.e. flexible in the sense that skills can be applied in transactions with any counterpart. Opportunities are fostered outside their established working relationships, and are not locked resources into specific partnerships. Adaptation is enforced through takeover, which provides control through internalization. Among the Japanese, in contrast, strong reputation effects and invisible links allow for trust without acquisition, resulting in investment and skills which are adjusted to specific counterparts without formal ownership and control.

Broadly speaking, there is likely to be some trade-off in the promotion of skills and abilities that are oriented towards compatibility with specific counterparts and those which are oriented towards efficient transactions in external markets with any counterparts. In the terminology of Kydland and Prescott (1977), a 'dynamic inconsistency' might then arise in the optimal plan of Western firms in Japan. *Ex ante*, a Western firm in Japan has an incentive to commit itself to a close and long-term relationship with a Japanese firm, in order to be accepted as a partner in the first place. *Ex post* a partnership has been established, however, it may be better for the Western firm to retain outside opportunities, as Westerners otherwise do, since its organization as a whole is oriented in this way (Andersson 1992b).

A certain firm may be expected to lose from teaming up with another if its skills are oriented towards that specific partnership while those of the other firm are not. In the West, Japanese firms may obtain knowledge about local conditions through acquisition. Alternatively, they may adapt to a generally lower level of commitment in informal relations. In Japan, on the other hand, it is less attractive to transform skills for occasional interactions with the few Westerners that are around. A Japanese firm then refrains from establishing a partnership unless some catch, or compensation, is involved. For example, interactions, from the Japanese perspective, may simply serve as a means to obtain technology. Oda and Grice (1988) report evidence of such behaviour by Japanese firms – meaning that partnerships are established, information is exchanged and partnerships are then dissolved. Alternatively, the volume of Western goods provided in this way would be kept sufficiently small to allow for high profits on the Japanese side.

It may be expected that possible credibility problems should be overcome when Western firms commit themselves to the Japanese economy. As found in the above-mentioned study by Odaka, however, foreign firms in Japan do not behave like domestic ones. The situation may change over time as the kind of options that Westerners offer will be more easily available for the Japanese. Employing qualified local workers, for example, appears to have become somewhat less difficult in the last few years. Some Japanese workers have begun to appreciate the 'Western options' of more rapid remuneration and changing employers without a loss of career opportunities. Nevertheless, it remains virtually impossible for foreign firms, especially those that are less well known, to attract personnel from the best Japanese universities.

Other explanations for the difficulties encountered by Westerners in Japan focus on the nature of competition. It is argued that Japanese firms collude in their home market, respect each others' market shares and avoid undercutting each others' price. Prices and profits therefore remain high in the domestic market and enable Japanese firms to dump products in the West, thereby achieving economies of scale. The result is large exports in the 'wrong' direction, from high-cost Japan to low-cost Western countries, whose producers might not be able to survive the Japanese dumping (Krugman 1984). In a general sense, however, the fierce competition which can be observed in Japan is an argument against such collusion. Ito *et al.* (1991) speak of excess competition between Japanese firms to export. With a low price elasticity in Japan, there would be upward pressure on prices at home, providing revenue which finances the long-term expansion of market shares abroad.

According to either perspective, prices remain high in the Japanese home market, allowing firms to finance exports abroad. Of course, the generally high price level is not necessarily evidence of barriers to foreign products. Komiya and Irie (1990) argue that consumer and retail prices are high because of a strong comparative advantage in tradeables, the relative price of which determines the exchange rate. The high land and labour costs do account for a large proportion of the costs for non-tradeables. However, this hardly explains the relatively high price, and limited supply, of Western products in Japan.

This chapter has discussed the internationalization of corporate activities and the characteristics of East Asian societies. An increasing share of world trade today occurs within industries, and within individual firms. On the basis of strategic considerations, multinational corporations are able to exploit country differences in costs, gain access to markets and technologies, and influence the economies in which they operate. The Japanese are now challenging the dominance of Western multinationals. Japan itself is characterized by a marked ability to establish commitments in human relations, which may be associated with the prevalence of a certain 'equilibrium'. This can be observed as structures marked by an intense exchange of information and the upgrading of skills which are well tailored to them. East Asia as a whole shares such characteristics, although each society has its special features as well. The internationalization of business operations in the region has contributed to its growth and export performance. Moreover, Japanese firms in particular have become successful within Western markets, while they so far retain core activities in R&D at home. In contrast, Western firms have problems both in exporting to Japan and investing there. These asymmetries in performance on the 'other side' are related to the varying approaches in human relations.

4

CONFLICTING TRADE POLICIES

Protectionism and 'super-gains' from trade

The economic advancement of East Asia has intensified the competitive pressure experienced by firms and countries around the world. This has triggered a need to restructure. At the same time, it has led to demands for protection. This chapter is concerned with the impact of these conflicting impulses on the formulation of trade policies.

It should be noted that trade is a multifaceted concept. Some trade takes the traditional form of exchange of goods between different economies. We have noted that services have generally become a critical component of production, and that foreign investment has restructured the premises for trade, allowing factors as well as goods to be transferred across national boundaries within individual firms. There is equally important trade between domestic actors. This may be inter-personal as well as inter-generational, as the future is affected by the savings and consumption decisions of today. Finally, there are forms of unmanaged trade which affect welfare although no monetary compensation is involved.

4.1 IMPACTS ON TRADE POLICY

There are many forces which contribute to the formation of trade policies pursued by countries, groups of countries or international institutions. At the present time, East Asian dynamism is undoubtedly one of the most important. Other countries have generally found it necessary to respond in policy terms to this challenge. Either they try to learn and benefit from the rise of East Asia, or they try to cover themselves.

This chapter considers a number of major influences on trade policies which are affected by East Asian dynamism. These are divided into six categories:

1 protectionist measures, in the United States as well as in Europe, to reduce competitive pressures;
2 protectionist threats, primarily by the United States, aimed at 'opening up' East Asian markets;
3 trade liberalization, undertaken by less developed countries in and out of the region, in order to improve competitive positions;
4 trade liberalization in the form of economic integration, in Europe, North America and to some extent in developing countries as well as in the Pacific Basin itself;
5 deregulation of domestic economies, mostly by previously state-planned countries but also in the West, in order to create or improve the functioning of markets (this includes institutional changes that facilitate participation in international trade);
6 pressures to take account of the environment, including calls for trade barriers and requests for the establishment of functioning markets for non-commercial services.

These developments in international trade policy are contradictory. In the late 1980s and early 1990s, the multilateral trade system weakened as the Uruguay Round dragged on for years. The United States in particular adopted a range of new protectionist measures and pressures against other, selected countries. The EC similarly instituted trade obstacles, not least those directed at East Asian countries and firms. An increasing percentage of international trade is now subjected to protectionist measures other than tariffs. At the same time, there is an intensive process of regional liberalization.

Protectionist pronouncements flourish particularly in the United States, whose changed role in this respect is the prime concern of the following discussion on protectionism. Of course, neither this country nor any other was ever completely free from isolationist forces. On the whole, however, the United States has taken on the responsibility as champion of free trade since the early nineteenth century. For this reason, its exit from that camp represents the most fundamental change in attitudes of the last decade.

4.2 PROBLEMS FOR THE UNITED STATES

In the 1980s, the United States shifted from being the world's largest creditor country to history's largest debtor. This reflected a worsening savings–investment balance and a deficit in the country's external trade. An already low level of private savings was now coupled with declining government savings. The process was triggered off in the early part of the decade by large tax cuts combined with increased public spending in order to finance higher military expenditures.

It may be argued that the debacle in Vietnam hurt America's perception of itself as 'guardian' of the 'free world'. Errors in the foreign policy of the Carter Administration, most conspicuously in its attempts to free the hostages in Iran, did not improve the situation. As the Reagan Administration came to power and the 'Iran problem' was immediately swept away, a relieving signal was radiated to the American people. The world had been mistaken in its attitudes. The time had come for the United States to take on undisputed leadership once again!

The following years were characterized by what has popularly been labelled 'Reaganomics'. Domestic demand boomed and imports grew more rapidly than exports. The dollar strengthened in spite of the trade deficit and the build-up of foreign debt. Interest rates remained at a reasonable level, mainly because foreigners reinvested in US securities. Troubled by the high level of costs at home, however, the industrial base weakened while other economies took advantage of the excessive US demand. In spite of worries for the consequences of the twin deficits, the Administration tried to resist attempts to reduce military expenditures. Raising taxes was out of the question.

This development brought the United States into substantial macroeconomic imbalance. However, there are difficulties for the United States at the microeconomic level as well. The United States remains the technological centre of the world, and possesses first class universities for the intellectual elite – which attract brilliant students from all over the world. Notwithstanding the presence of knowledge at the *frontier*, there is a shortage of production within the United States itself. As discussed in Chapter 2, US industry has steadily lost market shares across the entire industrial spectrum. Some explanations for this state of affairs, returned to below, have blamed foreigners, i.e. the Japanese. Leaving them aside for the moment, there is a general concern with the American model of business organization, especially compared with Japan and Germany.

Profits remain relatively high in many industries, although

comparisons with Japan and Germany are distorted owing to the considerably higher corporate income tax in these countries and more stable ownership structures, which make it less essential to report profits. Above all, the US economy does well in starting up new firms, and there is a great deal of flexibility and efficiency in the short term. Over the longer term, however, relatively few firms engage in continuous refinement and improvements, labour turn-over tends to be high, and corporate linkages come and go.

The overriding objective of US firms is to satisfy their share-holders. While managers must put a priority on communication with owners, there would appear to be limited flows of information within companies, as well as about companies among potential owners. Porter (1992) discusses how acquisition of existing firms is encouraged, since this concerns easily valued assets, at the expense of the internal development of intangible assets which are hard to evaluate by the market. There was also a weakening of antitrust legislation during the 1980s, reducing the deterrent for large-scale acquisitions of smaller firms. Accordingly, the risks of external takeover have grown substantially, contributing to short-term horizons and underinvestment in long-term projects.

In the past, military R&D stimulated US industry through spillovers to civilian activities. For various reasons, these gains have diminished. Military demands have shifted into a field of less economic relevance and there has been less emphasis on generic research in military programmes. More important, however, is the widespread concern about the management of technology in the civilian sector. Many collaborative ventures have been established in R&D in the last decade. Mowery (1992) notices that these focus on the exchange of already existing technology and marketing, rather than on the exploration of new options. This reflects the lower prevalence of information problems in the exchange of already existing knowledge compared with those involved in the development of new. It appears that the US economy has a wealth of activities in both invention and innovation, but lacks the structures and communication which are required to link the two fully.

There are more fundamental features of American economy and society which raise question marks regarding its long-term vitality. The high social and physical mobility accounts for a general state of anonymity among individuals. At the same time, the American way emphasizes 'freedom' for the individual. In some sense, this concept replaces the virtue of 'trust' in East Asia. In American society, there is relatively little basis for commitments in human relations. Mobility reduces the importance of reputation effects, while the emphasis on the priorities of the individual leads to minimal attention being paid to the welfare of groups. The result is a state of certain distrust, which must be compensated by efforts in supervision and monitoring (Casson 1990).

The drawbacks of this situation worsened in the 1980s when the burdened public sector had to look for feasible ways to scale down expenditures. The result was a squeeze on physical infrastructure as well as on social investment. Oddly enough, the United States still has the largest share of public expenditure spent on education. Health care also consumes a greater share of national income than in any other country. Nevertheless, the educational system has come under pressure, many inhabitants have lost secure access to health care, urban decay has become more prevalent, etc. Although services replace many of the jobs previously offered by manufacturing, the rate of unemployment has increased and real wages have fallen for the majority of the work force. The tax cuts, on the other hand, have provided mainly the wealthiest with more means.

These developments have accounted for growing inequalities and social tension. Heavy expenditure has to be made on insurance, lawyers, guns and alarm systems. For many women – the 'other half' of humanity – even home has turned into a dangerous and fearful place.[1] Racial minorities also bear a disproportionate share of the burdens that follow from less reliability and security. The 'American dilemma' laid out by Myrdal (1944) has attained new features, especially in the clusters of black people in the inner cities. The growing problems with crime and violence show up in the statistics on murder, rape, theft and the size of the prison population, as seen in Table 4.1. While several European countries also display high figures,[2] the difference in comparison with Japan is striking. Japan was well below the other countries in all respects except for the proportion of imprisoned citizens.

4.3 THE DIMINISHED GIANT SYNDROME

As the domestic economy ran into trouble during the 1980s, and the trade deficits refused to disappear, the United States imposed or negotiated a number of import restrictions. Countries in East

Table 4.1 Crime statistics

Country	Murder[a]	Rape[a]	Theft[a]	Imprisoned[b]
United States	9.4	41.2	5,345	381
Japan	1.0	1.3	1,170	88
Belgium	2.2	6.1	2,618	61
France	4.5	8.1	4,017	85
Germany, Federal Republic	3.9	8.2	4,351	153
Italy	6.4	–	2,800	43
UK	2.2	6.5	5,699	129
Spain	2.4	4.5	2,044	80
Sweden	7.0	16.4	8,618	98

Sources: Interpol 1992; United Nations 1991
Notes: [a] Number of crimes reported in 1990 per 100,000 inhabitants.
[b] Per 100,000 in 1986.

Asia were commonly the targets. Antidumping and countervailing duties, rather than voluntary export restraints (VERs) and orderly market agreements (OMAs), became the key instruments. This tendency shows a significantly weakened commitment to multilateralism, and a movement towards bilateralism as well as unilateralism. This is most ominous in the arbitrary 'fair trade' provisions such as 'Regular 301' and 'Super 301'. There are also vociferous calls for 'managed trade' with demands for reciprocity, not in opportunities but in 'results'. These 'results' would come from sweeping East Asian structural reforms to accommodate US exporters.

Two parallel trade policy 'discussions' have been going on between Washington and Tokyo in the last few years – the Super 301 negotiations, and the Structural Impediments Initiative. Under the Super 301 provision, the Administration must report to Congress in the spring of each year and identify countries for bilateral negotiations aimed at removing specific trade barriers which damage US exports. Japan, together with India and Brazil, was cited under 301 in 1989. Bilateral discussions with Japan have dealt with import barriers to foreign satellites, supercomputers, semiconductors, and forest and agricultural products.

Of course, the United States does not speak with one voice, and the Administration is typically less protectionistic than Congress. The former takes total interests – not just vested interests – into account. It therefore has stronger incentives to avoid confrontation with Japan, which is a power with considerable influence on macro policy conditions. Under both Reagan and Bush, the Administration emphasized efforts to open East Asian markets rather than close the United States, thus threatening protection to avoid protection. Carla Hills, US trade representative, defended Super 301 as a market opening, non-protectionist device.

In practice, Regular 301 as well as Super 301 represent dangerous interventions in trade not because of what they do to US export policy but because of what they do to import policy. Their effect is to disarm the old option of a president to call for 'export policies' as a means of doing away with protectionist pressure in the United States. '301' arms a president not with the authority to remove US import restrictions but with the authority to impose new ones. It provides the vehicle to press for export expansion without paying the price of removing US import restrictions.

Protectionist measures might have been provided with a rationale from 'strategic trade theory' (Brander and Spencer 1985; Krugman 1986). Given increasing returns to scale, product differentiation and imperfect competition, the simplicity of models based on perfectly competitive markets disappears. A country may then gain from subsidizing oligopolistic firms, thereby enabling them to get an upper hand on foreign competitors. Similar to the arguments for optimum tariffs, however, it is not easy to apply strategic trade policy in reality, or to master its consequences. The theory does not tell us under what circumstances interventionist policies are effective, how large the gains may be, or whether policy makers possess the information required to handle them. The risks of retaliation raise further issues, and may fuel spirals of punitive and costly actions, leaving everyone much worse off than they were at the outset.[3]

Other arguments have focused on the role of foreign direct investment. The United States has been a prime actor in this field for a long time. Up to the 1980s, the country was responsible for an indisproportionately large share of the outflows, while in the 1980s it became the dominant destination for the inflows – accounting for about half of the world's total. The technology transfers which followed from both outward and inward investment flows have been criticized. However, the US outflows have been found to enhance the R&D capacity of US firms, without any significant leakage to competitors (Mansfield and Romeo 1980; Mansfield *et al.* 1983).

Controls on outflows of US technology, on the other hand, reduced US competitiveness according to Hawkins and Gladwin

(1980). The problems that have been found concern the adaptability of multinationals in general, and United States ones in particular, to the local conditions in host countries (Reddy and Zhao 1990). These would mainly reduce the welfare effects on the host countries, while the multinational firms become less effective than they would have been with such adaptation. From this it does not follow, however, that they become less efficient than they would have done without the direct investment.

The inflows of foreign direct investment to the United States in the 1980s, in contrast to previous periods, were mainly financed from abroad. This is what would be expected with the low level of earnings in the United States at the time. Great Britain accounted for the largest stock in 1990 calculated on a historical cost basis, with Japan responsible for about 20 per cent.[4] However, the Japanese net flow in 1990 amounted to 47 per cent of the total. Furthermore, the Japanese firms are particularly important in terms of sales, as a good deal of their investment targets wholesale trading (Lipsey 1992).

As discussed in the preceding chapter, Japanese firms both establish new ventures and acquire already existing companies in the United States. The latter facilitate entry and enable the acquisition of valuable management know-how. Both categories are generally received with praise by the communities and states which obtain them. Their entry often revitalizes ailing industries and provides new jobs. Encarnation (1992) argues that the Japanese act in the United States similarly to how US and Japanese firms act in other countries. The difference, according to him, is in the options that confront US firms in Japan.

The Japanese acquisition and withdrawal of US technology is more controversial. However, the problems in US industry are not caused by the entry of the Japanese but by its own inability to apply basic research effectively in commercial production. It has been argued that the fragmentation of US industries impedes the application of sophisticated technological systems. In the semiconductor industry and related capital equipment, for example, only two major US producers have remained leaders for many years – Texas Instruments and Motorola. According to Ferguson (1988), most of the industry consists of small firms characterized by high personnel turnover, little personnel training, insufficient economies of scale and avoidance of long-term cooperative inter-firm relationships.

Obstacles and frictions impede flows of information between those who develop technology and those who apply it.

Protectionist policies, whether they target exports to the United States or try to limit or shut out foreign investment, cannot be expected to cure either the US trade deficit or its domestic problems. As long as the United States uses more resources through consumption and investment than it produces, the balance must inevitably be achieved through an influx of capital from abroad and must show up as a deficit on the current account. In fact, US national investment net of depreciation did not show any major decline in the 1980s, while the national savings ratio did. Japan, like Germany through most of the 1980s, became the natural supplier of capital to the United States. This was because their national investment ratios declined more than their savings ratios, leaving them with a surplus. At the same time, their industries provided a great proportion of the imports that the United States was demanding.

One might ask, then, for the real reason behind the change in US trade policies. What Bhagwati (1989) calls 'the diminished giant syndrome' probably provides the best explanation. The United States has lost its previous economic dominance, partly through the rise of Japan and the ANIEs, and partly as a result of its own policies. National interest groups focusing on the necessity of retaining this or that industry, or nurturing new industries, will inevitably exert their influence. The balance of payments deficits recorded by the United States in the bilateral trade with Japan, and the continuing takeover of well-known and fashionable industries, make it easy to see why 'Japan-bashing' has become attractive in Washington. The deindustrialization that took place during the years of an overvalued dollar, together with the inequalities and social problems aggravated by the lowered taxes and cuts in non-military expenditure, now fuel such sentiments. Finally, the fall of the Soviet empire has reduced the number of foreign scapegoats available to blame for domestic problems.

The concomitant change in attitudes should come as no surprise when viewed in a historical perspective. Balance of payments difficulties have given rise to protectionist activities in the past as well. When Great Britain, for example, was the prime economic power in the nineteenth century, 'its policy of fair field and no favour was also a minimal restatement of the political conditions for economic hegemony' (Lipson 1985). By the time of the Great

Depression (1873–94), the diminution in Britain's pre-eminence had begun. This led to a rise in protectionist sentiments and demands for an end to Britain's unilateral embrace of free trade principles. 'Fair trade and reciprocity' became promoted by the National Fair Trade League, the National Society for the Defence of British Industry and the Reciprocity Fair Trade Association. Today, the United States follows the same path. The United States and Germany were to Britain what the Pacific nations – and Japan in particular – are now to the United States.

To the extent that the United States still sets patterns, these developments are threatening. Agricultural policies are nowadays a mess of restrictions encountered in most industrialized countries. However, there is considerable resistance to solving the problems, and conflicts have virtually paralysed the Uruguay Round for years. The story may be traced back to US unilateral action to introduce quotas on dairy products in 1950, and on other products in 1951. These policies, legalized by the United States, were happily copied by others with unhappy results. Similarly, the United States legalized protectionism in textiles through a VER with Japan in 1957. An instrument was thereby created which has been used over and over again by the United States itself as well as by others across a wide range of goods, in spite of its highly detrimental effects on social welfare.

In the postwar period, US support for free trade and an orderly investment regime has still been much more important than its deviations. As the United States no longer exercises this important leadership, but instead sets destructive examples, the consequences will be far-reaching. This has been pointed out, for example, in a statement by forty leading US economists, among them four Nobel Laureates and four former chairmen of the Council of Economic Advisers in the US Administration (*World Economy* 1989).

The arbitrariness of a major power which seeks its own *ad hoc* advantage rather than a set of rules – the application of which it would be willing to reciprocate when the tables are turned – has always created deep animosities. It has been argued that international order is a public good which must emanate from a single leading nation (Kindleberger 1969). Gilpin (1975) maintained that, historically, a stable liberal order has been the creation of a succession of hegemonies. He predicted that the weakened US position would cause general instability and uncertainty in the world economy. On the other hand, Keohane and Nye (1977) disputed that shifts in hegemonic power would be reflected in variations in the international structure of issues. The nationalizations of foreign-owned equity in the early 1970s similarly did not cease as a result of hegemony, but rather because of the changing nature of interactions between host countries and multinational companies mentioned in Chapter 3.

4.4 'OPENING UP' JAPAN

The prevalence of the US savings–investment deficit, and other domestic problems, does not rule out that 'opening up' East Asian markets would be beneficial. It has been noted that, although certain unfair trade barriers remain, the ANIEs as well as Japan have gradually liberalized their trade regimes. Japan probably has fewer government-controlled trade obstacles than most other countries. Attention has instead been focused on 'informal, or 'invisible', barriers to trade and investment. In particular, the United States has pushed for the Structural Impediments Initiative, a programme aimed at identifying and removing factors within Japan itself which prevent the sales of foreign products.

Above all, Washington wants Japan to reform its multi-layer distribution system to facilitate sales of foreign products. Criticism has focused on the 1974 law on the adjustment of retail business activity in large-scale retail stores.[5] Among other requirements are rationalized land use to make more land available for construction purposes, increased infrastructure investment, stricter anti-cartel laws and loosened company groups – *keiretsu* – to discourage excluding business practices (such as bid rigging, price fixing, group boycott and market allocation), improved protection of intellectual property rights (for instance by speeding up processes for granting foreigners patent protection) and reduced working hours as well as savings in favour of more leisure time and more consumption-oriented attitudes.

Tokyo has retorted by asking the United States to deal at long last with its budget deficit, reduce excessive consumption and promote savings, increase the availability of risk capital, and improve the educational system to enhance competitiveness. In spite of an apparent uneasiness about the US demands, the Japanese authorities appear to be making efforts to respond favourably. After the Bush–Kaifu meeting in California in 1990, Kaifu promised to 'firmly tackle structural reforms of Japan as one of the top priorities of my cabinet, with a view to improving the quality of Japanese life with further stress on the consumer-oriented society' (*International Herald Tribune* 1990a).

The structural reforms that have been requested, however, are outside the control of the usual expenditure switches and adjustments which make up the ordinary macroeconomic kit. Their undertaking involves fundamental alterations of Japanese life and generates, almost by definition, strong political resistance. When Kaifu met with his countrymen after the mentioned meeting, the press reported 'harsh criticism greets Kaifu on return from Bush talks' (*International Herald Tribune* 1990b). The United States itself has been unable to deliver on numerous international undertakings, even within the Structural Impediments Initiative discussions with Japan. Still, redressing the US economic imbalances would take much less disconcerting measures, and could be managed through the conventional method of macroeconomic policies.

Impatient with the pace at which Japan is 'restructured', the United States has repeatedly raised more specific demands on what the Japanese should do. As a result of US pressure, some 30 per cent of the Japanese computer chip market has been declared the 'domain of US producers'. A trip by Bush and presidents of the American automobile producers in the spring of 1992 resulted in a promise that the Japanese would buy some US$30 billion of American automobiles and automobile components over the following years. When approached by representatives from other countries, MITI and the Japanese automobile industry explained that this was not an example of managed trade. The Japanese companies had merely 'revealed their purchasing plans'.

The previous chapter discussed possible explanations for the high prices of Western products in Japan. First, there may be an overlapping of information on the Japanese side which puts Western counterparts at a disadvantage. Second, credibility problems may arise because of the lesser inclination on the Western side to commit capacities and skills to specific counterparts. Third, there may be tacit collusion between Japanese firms at home or, alternatively, excessive competition to export.

Whichever is correct, all these interpretations raise doubts concerning the virtues of forcing the Japanese to make deals with foreigners. Asymmetric handling of information may merely lead to more deals which are unprofitable for Westerners and credibility problems are likely to be worsened. Regarding the nature of competition among Japanese firms, it is far from clear how this is affected by 'forced business'. Collusive behaviour may be enforced to counter such attacks. Beyond this, incentives which facilitate the entry of certain investments at the expense of others are inefficient. The same applies to the undertaking of activities which would not be sustainable even without any bias against them in the Japanese market. Furthermore, 'forcing' the Japanese to buy 'foreign' leads to less effort on the part of Westerners to adjust themselves to the special features of Japan.

There may still be a case for intervention to facilitate the entry of foreign firms in Japan. Each Western firm which succeeds in establishing itself exposes the Japanese to 'opportunities of the Western kind'. This goes for potential employees, suppliers, distributors, consumers, etc. By providing locals with more options outside the traditional realm, this may make it slightly easier for other newcomers to be accepted as employers or business partners. Exclusive Japanese relations, which keep prices up and wages down until old age, may consequently be undermined. The implication is that each foreign entry in Japan will be associated with a favourable external effect on the possibilities of entry for other Western firms. No matter how real such an effect may be, it is not taken into account by individual companies. This cannot be used, however, as support for measures which worsen the situation further.

It deserves to be asked, of course, whether entry by foreigners, and whatever dissolution of the traditional Japanese system that might bring, is desirable for Japan. Although this question must ultimately be left to be answered by the Japanese, certain observations can be made. Given a sufficiently great presence of Westerners, the Japanese 'equilibrium' might to some extent break down. That outcome could also be triggered by acquaintance with foreigners by Japanese travelling and living abroad. In fact, there are many observations that such growing international experience does have a strong impact, especially on Japanese children who are enrolled in foreign schools. Many 'overseas Japanese' experience considerable problems in making a readjustment when they return, but it will probably take time before this has any profound impact on Japan itself.

An 'internationalization' of the Japanese economy should not necessarily make it less efficient, as seen from the ability of the Japanese to apply their skills abroad. There ought to be reduced prices in Japan, however, which would provide less financing for expansion abroad. Even if such a scenario might have unwanted cultural effects, and may be undesirable for industry in a short-term perspective, it should benefit consumers. There are additional reasons why entry by foreigners, and accepting them as business partners, might represent the best possible avenue for the Japanese society, especially in the long run. The world is becoming increasingly interdependent, and a one-sided build-up of Japanese assets and control over foreign production might not be accepted and honoured by others in the end.

There are other possible scenarios, of course. The Japanese may find that scaling down their activities and sales in Western markets would be a way of avoiding excessively large imbalances and political frictions. This could then be replaced by an enhanced expansion on their part within the East Asian region, which would become even more dominated by intra-regional flows. The rest of the world, the 'outskirts of the West', would be 'left to itself'. Another, less awesome, scenario from a Western perspective takes the demographic change in Japan as its point of departure. With more elderly people in the future, Japanese savings rates may come down and consumption increase. This might also be supported by more spending-oriented behaviour among the younger generation. The Japanese trade surplus may then disappear in due time and be replaced by surpluses for countries which are at present developing and are often highly indebted. With such a course of events, the Japanese savings and trade surplus is nothing to worry about, much less to complain about.

The fact is that the world is plagued by a scarcity of capital, and more so today than only a decade ago. Millions of workers are unemployed all over the world, not least in the United States and in Europe. In Japan and Western economies alike, prices on equity have fallen considerably since the spending days of the 1980s, and it will take time for the financial systems to recover. Restructuring the Russian Republic and other formerly planned and now devastated economies will require enormous investment. This is not to say that money should be provided as a gift. On the contrary, a reasonably reliable and stable situation must be established before external finance can make any meaningful contribution. However, other countries must make a real effort to offer technological assistance, education and training which can help to establish preconditions for development. Once orderly conditions are in place, external financing is likely to be both needed and attracted on a large scale. In developing countries, there is an equally huge demand for capital. Reversing the current mismanagement of the environment will similarly require vast amounts of investment. The only significant source of funds at the present time is high-saving Japan. In this situation, is it reasonable, is it even excusable, to ask that the Japanese cut their savings and start consuming? Where is the capital to come from?

To the extent that Japan does manage to get rid of its internal obstacles to trade, there will be a boost to its competitiveness. Capital and labour would be reallocated from low productivity use in agriculture, services and the distribution system to efficient export industries. For this reason, outside pressure is welcomed by many policy makers in Japan, intent on undertaking structural reforms that are to their advantage under all circumstances. The US pressures to 'open up' Japan may remind us of Commodore Perry's arrival in 1853, and the enormous increase in Japanese competitiveness that followed.

4.5 'SUPER-GAINS' FROM TRADE

In the best of all possible worlds, the model of free trade assures us that unlimited competition is in everyone's interest. For this reason, and to prevent large countries from discriminating against small ones, there is in theory at least a more or less universal adherence to the principle of 'multilateralism'. Within the framework of the GATT, there have been substantial reductions in tariff rates since the Second World War. After successive rounds of multilateral negotiations, the average most-favoured-nation (MFN) rates on manufactured products in developed countries have been reduced from some 40 per cent in the 1940s to 6 per cent in 1990.

Estimates of the gains from trade through elimination of tariffs, for instance in a European customs union, have produced fairly modest effects. However, the tendency towards protectionism concerns not tariffs but non-tariff barriers (NTBs). This is the case even though NTBs are generally much more damaging to social welfare in the country which adopts them. As has been calculated, e.g. in the Cecchini (1988) report for the EC, the abolishment of NTBs is likely to be associated with major economic gains. The reason they are still instituted, and maintained, is that they enable small groups of well-organized producers to capture large profits, while the losses are spread thinly among large numbers of consumers. Hence, the effects tend to be detrimental from an equity perspective as well.

Many NTBs take the form of both border and non-border measures. For example, there are controls which impose domestic taxes, various sorts of inspection procedures, protectionist rules for public procurement, transport, telecommunications, market access, etc. The costs of NTBs show up as an inferior allocation of resources, smaller economies to scale, reduced competition and more cumbersome macroeconomic problems. In addition, modern protectionism is often selective in nature, targeting not only certain industries and countries but individual firms and even specific products. This means, for example, that the range of available product varieties is limited, which is a major issue for the highly differentiated consumer goods supplied by Japanese firms (cars, consumer electronics, etc.). Adverse effects on the choice of quality lead to additional losses.

It is often difficult to observe the real impact of protectionism, especially for the selective kind. It may be the threat, rather than the policy itself, which hurts. In the case of antidumping proceedings, Messerlin (1989) found that imported quantities were reduced by 40 per cent three years after the initiation of investigations and an average *ad valorem* equivalent of some 23 per cent. According to Prusa (1992), the adverse effects are even greater when the policy is withdrawn than when it is carried out. The negotiated outcomes, agreed upon to avoid duties, are worse for the consumers, and for social welfare, than the duties themselves. There are also great losses for those countries and firms which are targeted by protectionism. Trela and Whalley (1988) estimated that all developing countries lose some US$8 billion per annum owing to the restrictiveness of the textile quotas and tariffs adopted by industrialized countries through the Multifiber Arrangement. In addition, there are losses within developing countries which arise as a result of the inefficient allocation of export licences.

It is true that we need much more research on the connections between trade and the processes which lie behind technological progress and innovation, as noted by Grossman and Helpman (1990) among others. However, the East Asian success with an outward-oriented development strategy and application of various technologies has focused attention on gains from trade which go beyond the basic models. The following 'super-gains' from trade can be added to those normally put forward in the literature.

- A commitment to an expansion of trade in a growing number of countries reduces the risks in investment oriented towards the world market, and facilitates an efficient allocation of resources internationally.

- More trade enables a larger scale of production, which helps to bear fixed costs for improvements in technologies, training, production methods and marketing, and makes improvements more profitable. As a result of international trade it also becomes more costly not to upgrade production processes and product concepts. With a greater number of competitors there is a bigger risk of being outclassed by others engaged in search to a greater extent.[6]

- Experience of foreign markets necessitates and facilitates efforts to adjust products and increase the flexibility of production processes, organizational structures and management practices. Through a feedback of information, this makes the entire organization of firms more efficient.

- Contact with foreign producers, abroad or at home, brings confrontation with new kinds of innovation and application of technology. Domestic firms must put greater efforts into meeting the demands of purchasers and consumers, and upgrade the capabilities of the work force.

- The increased presence of foreign products in the home market provides consumers with more alternatives, making them more conscious about differences in quality. This adds further pressure on domestic producers to improve output.

- Both management and employees become accustomed to adjustment needs and try to handle them by acting rather than reacting. Consequently they engage less in 'directly unproductive activities', i.e. spending resources on persuading governments to provide protection and privileges.

- When gains from trade are recognized, governments are more likely to accept change and withstand any domestic pressures seeking escape from adjustment.

- An open economy is more exposed to international economic disturbances, but also better equipped to handle shocks. A large export sector can more easily be expanded and imports more easily contracted. At the same time, the government is better prepared to apply macroeconomic tools of adjustment. By contrast, income levels in an import substituting country are often too low to reduce. This means that it is mainly essentials that are

87

imported, i.e. costly input goods which are necessary to keep the expensive and inefficient production going. These differences were highlighted by the varying performance of countries during the oil crises of the 1970s.

• Undistorted markets account for positive employment effects in less developed countries, as labour-intensive production methods replace the high capital intensity of import substitution. Together with the contraction of scarcity rents to capital owners, this favours a more equitable income distribution without compromising incentives.

• If one can conduct business without constant contacts with the government, it is easier to survive in the provinces. This has a positive effect on the regional distribution of production, which contributes to smaller income differences overall.

Regarding protectionist policies, countries pursue not only tariffs and NTBs but also what we may call 'domestic trade barriers' (DTBs). These take many forms, such as subsidies, zoning laws, economic planning in general, restrictive practices by unions and corporations, and limitations on the right of establishment. They could be put into effect by governments or by firms, groups of firms or unions. Regulating trade is normally neither the aim nor the immediate consequence of DTBs. Their effects on international trade appear indirectly, and sometimes in a way which makes it difficult to classify a regulation as an NTB or a DTB. Yet, the distinction can usually be made. For example, a rule preventing the establishment of foreign banks is an NTB, while a regulation prohibiting banks from owning an insurance company is a DTB.

Tariffs and NTBs give rise to smuggling across national borders. DTBs set up similar forces. There is 'smuggling' in the form of tax evasion and the development of an underground economy. The more constrained this 'smuggling' is, the more 'home' production there will be. The theoretical trade models usually assume free domestic trade and then explore the consequences of international trade, i.e. the removal of tariffs and NTBs. This may obscure important relationships. There is often a substantial amount of high DTBs even in countries with strong support for the idea of free trade.

In the same way as DTBs will ultimately have an effect on foreign trade, international trade also has an impact on DTBs. Tariffs and NTBs are eliminated through unilateral decisions, negotiations, cross-country agreements or foreign pressure of various kinds. The domestic financial market, for example, may be opened to foreign banks because it is necessary for the national banks to be permitted to establish offices or affiliates abroad. DTBs may be similarly exposed to foreign pressures. Normally, however, other countries are likely to accept 'national treatment', i.e. they accept domestic obstacles to trade which do not discriminate against foreigners. DTBs which are the result of private operations are also relatively difficult to combat by government decisions. Hence, DTBs must often be removed by other mechanisms.

As a direct result of international trade, foreign competition is able to dismantle some DTBs. This may help to undermine some domestic monopolies and restrictive practices. Olson (1982) sets out reasons why 'distributional alliances' may be harder to operate in a wider market. Nevertheless, most DTBs are not undone in this direct way.

A number of government DTBs could be eradicated through unilateral decision (deregulation) in order to increase the international competitiveness of the economic system as a whole, or to improve the bargaining power of certain branches relative to their international competitors. A country may, for instance, negotiate the elimination of NTBs in order to prevent the establishment of foreign insurance companies. In order not to put national insurance corporations at an impossible competitive disadvantage, it may be necessary as the next step to undo DTBs in the insurance business. A country which abolishes its foreign exchange restrictions may similarly find it advantageous to reduce taxes on capital market transactions. The more mobile factors are across borders, the greater the likelihood that domestic forces will do away with obstacles to domestic trade in an effort to retain international competitiveness.

Openness to trade brings pressures that help to identify obstacles to efficiency as well as generate the political power to combat the groups that gain from them. Thus, international trade may remove internal obstacles and thereby revitalize an economy from within.

The removal of DTBs will generally be desirable from a social point of view. Domestic trade is as important as international trade, and gains from domestic trade are basically the same as those from international trade. This section has demonstrated the prevalence of 'super-gains', which add another dimension to the ordinary economic benefits of trade. Paving the way for more constructive and creative institutions, trade contributes to the dynamic processes of change. It should be noted, however, that some DTBs may establish useful regulations of trade. For example, there are goods and services whose production or consumption is associated with negative externalities.

4.6 INTERNATIONAL MOVEMENTS TOWARDS TRADE LIBERALIZATION

In parallel with the pressure for protectionism, there are continuous and successful movements in favour of liberalization. The new protectionism sometimes appears to dominate only because, on the whole, trade barriers are removed under other headings. However, the most conspicuous struggle for liberalization, the Uruguay Round, has run into severe difficulties. The truth is that the Uruguay Round represents by far the most ambitious project in the history of GATT. An effort on this scale became necessary because of the rapid restructuring of both international trade and trade policies pursued by countries.

Among other things, the Uruguay Round has attempted the following: first, to bring new issues under the umbrella of GATT, including particularly trade in services, patents and rules for policies with regard to foreign investments; second, to recapture the fields of agricultural products and clothes and textiles, which were disentangled from GATT many years ago; third, to reconsider the rules for various NTBs, such as antidumping policies and counter-vailing duties. Resolving these matters would in many cases invoke considerable costs on certain countries, and especially on vested interests within those countries. On the other hand, countries which experience high costs from certain actions benefit from others, which should have opened the door for compromises early on.

Instead, agricultural policies became the stumbling block which postponed any solution. This is quite astonishing, given the enormous costs that they have inflicted not only on the countries with competitive advantages in agricultural production, such as the United States, Australia and developing countries, but also for taxpayers, particularly in the EC and Japan. European farmers, and especially French farmers, have staunchly defended the subsidies which back up their way of life. If and when the Uruguay Round finally reaches a conclusion, the outcome is likely to be weakened by political rigidities and may therefore not provide any real guarantee against the new kind of protectionism.

The success which the East Asian countries have recorded with outward-oriented strategies has increased the interest of less developed countries in the Round. On the other hand, the third world favours the right of each country to maintain whatever policies it prefers, adding further strains to the negotiations. Except for agricultural products, the Uruguay Round is actually not a top priority for the majority of developing countries. The East Asian demonstration effect makes less developed countries look for unilateral reductions instead, insisting that they should be exempted from the normal standards of the GATT discipline.

In fact, there is a strong tendency towards unilateral reductions of barriers in general. Some current developments are as follows.

- A number of industrial countries have made unilateral reductions in DTBs in order to increase domestic benefits, but also to raise their international competitiveness, especially in services.
- The East European countries are moving unilaterally towards liberalization, particularly in their DTBs. The elimination of DTBs is likely to be followed by reductions in tariffs and NTBs, probably with concessions by other countries to begin with. For example, the East European countries should gradually be accorded MFN treatment and become members of GATT (which some are already, but only in name).
- East Asian countries are in the process of reducing tariffs and NTBs partly as a result of foreign demands, partly to give a sharper edge to their already successful trade strategies. The Structural Impediments Initiative represents merely one interesting example of strong international pressure on DTBs. Again, the Japanese themselves would benefit from many of the reforms as entry would be generally facilitated.
- The most important removal of NTBs, however, occurs as part of the efforts to achieve economic integration on a regional basis. The most pervasive examples are the transformation of the Common Market in Europe into the Single Market, and the establishment of the North American Free Trade Agreement (NAFTA). The former, which encompasses a large number of relatively small and previously highly segmented economies, has been paralleled by unilateral reductions in DTBs. Intentionally or unintentionally, the EC has provided itself with an unexceptional

capacity not only to dissolve DTBs but also to introduce new ones. The misgivings of Mrs Thatcher about yielding authority to Brussels were probably not primarily motivated by a concern that the EC would adopt external barriers to trade. The most immediate risks may be associated with the issuing of excessively ambitious – i.e. restrictive – European-wide DTBs by the central authorities.

While regional integration is likely to continue in Europe and North America, what about the development in the Pacific? In fact, there have been many steps in that direction in this region as well. The countries in ASEAN grouped themselves together as early as 1965. Their cooperation has been successful in political terms, which was perhaps the primary objective, while the economic output has been meagre. The countries' heterogeneity and, at the same time, competition between them in trade and for the attraction of investment has prevented any major success as far as economic integration is concerned. The recent declarations of ASEAN to form AFTA, a Free Trade Association for these countries, have consequently not been much noticed in the rest of the world. For similar reasons, efforts to establish any palpable convergence of trade policies in greater parts of the Pacific Basin have so far yielded fora for general political and economic discussions rather than concrete results.

Being on the periphery, Australia is especially interested in expanded activities in the Pacific. Its possible loyalties with the West have been reduced by the agriculture and coal policies of the EC, which have cost Australia dearly. It is true that the country pursues discriminatory trade practices against East Asia, but it seems willing to correct such matters. The efforts of the Prime Minister, Mr Hawke, led to the formation of a 'non-treaty organization' in the Asian Pacific in 1989. This has been viewed as a sign of how far integration could realistically reach in the Pacific region within the foreseeable future.

There are several reasons for scepticism with regard to the realism of increased economic integration and cooperation in the Pacific Basin. As already mentioned, there is fear of too much dependence on Japan, which is still much more dominating in this part of the world in economic terms than, for example, Germany is in the EC. As pointed out in *Japan Times* in memory of Germany's 'peace chancellor' Willy Brandt, no Japanese leader has like him been able to heal the wounds of the cruelties of the war (*Japan Times* 1992). The countries in the Asian Pacific may also be claimed to be 'too' fierce competitors in foreign markets as well as 'too' complementary for the resource-rich countries to accept a Free Trade Area (Anderson 1991). Finally, there are concerns about the prospects of becoming too interlinked within a region which may eventually become dominated by China.

In spite of such counterarguments, the current trends may reverse the outlook sooner than is commonly thought. This is partly due to the introversion of North America and the EC, together with question marks concerning their future economic performance. These factors both raise the benefits and reduce the external costs of East Asian regionalism. As argued by Bergsten (1991), trade diversion is not merely a negative effect of regional liberalization, but actually an explicit goal. The Far East may need to unite in order to counteract discrimination in Western markets. Perhaps more important, Western economies may anyway become less crucial for ambitious East Asian exporters and investors.

East Asian countries attach a smaller weight to external opportunities relative to those that prevail among their neighbours, because of developments within the region itself. We have already observed the rapid growth in intra-regional trade. Meanwhile, there is less antagonism now between various actors within the region. Together with the economic progress, this has allowed several countries to adopt a more confident stance in their foreign policies. The ANIEs and the members of ASEAN play an increasingly active role, while Australia is already in favour of regional integration. Vietnam and the smaller countries in Indochina hardly pose any military threat any longer, but hunger for expanded relations. In Cambodia, Japan has pursued an unusually bold foreign policy, taking on a major responsibility in the still pending attempts to restore democracy and economic stability.

However, the most crucial developments in this context are taking place in China. That country is now determined to pursue economic reform – which is timely as 1997, and the ending of Hong Kong's special status, approaches. New links are established between the former enemies in Seoul and Beijing. We have seen that China has an intense economic exchange with Taipei through Hong Kong, although the political bonds are invisible. Tokyo probably has ambiguous feelings about the course of events. The maturing of its Asian neighbours creates just the counterweight that is needed

for them to take decisive steps towards enhanced regional cooperation although it occurs primarily through informal linkages rather
than formal treaties. While this opens up new opportunities for Japan,
it also invites a competition which may be fiercer than desired.

In order to develop, China needs extended commercial relations
with the more industrialized countries in East Asia, including not
only Japan but also the NIEs. China's demands will be positively
responded to by East Asia, not least because its stability is a
precondition for the prosperity of the region as a whole. In
addition, the overseas Chinese know how to conduct business in
China, and how to exploit the opportunities that abound in its
capable and inexpensive labour force. Tokyo cannot afford to stand
aside from this development, although its participation will enable
China to fulfil its tremendous potential more quickly, and thereby
move towards a predominant position in the Pacific Basin. Together
with the growing competitiveness of the region, these tensions make
it unlikely that any regional convergence would motivate a desire
to discriminate against outsiders. On the contrary, Japan as well as
the other countries in East Asia would be unhappy with regional
integration at the expense of external relations. Whether they
possess the initiative to take affirmative action actually to defend an
open world trade system is another thing.

The general processes of regional liberalization will hardly be
reversed whatever the course of the multilateral trading system.
However, a successful Uruguay Round would crucially diminish
the risks. Given that outsiders are not discriminated against, there
are great advantages with regional integration. The dissolution of
market segmentation not only enhances the efficiency of a region,
but makes it more accessible for outsiders as well. Bhagwati (1991)
suggests that regional agreements should be more fully incorporated
in GATT. One of the major challenges for the years ahead is
undoubtedly to reduce the scope for trade diversion and make
regional liberalization compatible with free trade in general.

4.7 THE UNRECORDED COMMONS

While there are advantages with a 'bigger world', there may be
disadvantages as well, because the physical and ecological framework that encloses human societies is not becoming bigger at all.
As long as our planet, with its pools of natural resources and scenic
beauty, had vast dimensions relative to the scope of human activities,

there was little reason to take account of effects on the environment. However, the economic system and the number of humans keep growing.

As the world ceases to be endless, the unguided and unconstrained use of the environment starts to be costly. The environment provides services which are 'non-commercial' and 'collective goods' for which it is difficult to claim ownership. This is not to say that environmental values are less tangible than commercial goods. Air to breathe and water to drink represent infrastructure which is fundamental for all economic activities, as for life itself. At the same time, it is often difficult to evaluate environmental effects with certainty before it may be too late. This makes it necessary to specify charges by weighing risks against each other.

Mismanagement of the environment involves, in effect, 'trade' which is unmanaged by compensating payments. Environmental effects on countries, generations and individuals are not unrelated to the prevalence of commercial trade. Daly (1968) argued that commercial trade is a major cause of environmental destruction. By speeding up the economic specialization of locations and increasing the intensity of industrial activities, it may enhance both the vulnerability of ecosystems and the pressure they are subjected to. Costanza (1992) has called for the adoption of 'ecological barriers' to commercial trade to take account of environmental costs and benefits. In essence, barriers to trade would compensate for the lack of compensation for environmental effects. On the other hand, economic specialization typically brings higher incomes, which has been suggested to increase the appreciation of environmental values as well as the availability of financing for pollution abatement. It has also been pointed out that 'environmentalists' risk becoming the prisoners of traditional 'protectionists', who look for any arguments to back up their interests (Hillman and Ursprung 1992).

The tropical forest is an example of a renewable natural resource which produces both non-commercial and commercial values. The absorption of CO_2 benefits the world as a whole, and especially countries like The Netherlands, Bangladesh and the Pacific Island states, which could more or less disappear with an increased greenhouse effect and a rising sea level. Genetic diversity similarly provides all countries with options for new food, medicines and other products. At the same time, lack of capital and technology prevents the producing countries from establishing industries for processing timber products. While the potential value of the information inherent in genetic diversity grows with the maturing of biotechnology, those who manage the forests may experience a declining ability to appropriate it.[7] Simply burning the forest or cutting and exporting logs may then be preferable to retaining future opportunities which the country might not be able to exploit anyway. Still, the producer countries obtain only a fraction of the commercial gains from the current exploitation of tropical forest. Most accrue to the consumer countries, mainly Japan and the EC (International Tropical Timber Organization 1991).

Wells (1992) points out that the costs of preserving forests tend to fall heavily on the local level, while the benefits are collected mostly at the global level. In addition, the benefits of preservation fall on future generations, who cannot speak today. An 'optimal' management of environmental values will in principle require that those responsible are confronted with the true costs and benefits which pertain to their actions. Accomplishing functioning 'trade' in all respects is not a realistic alternative, however. Restricting commercial trade will not do, since this hurts income and may reduce the appreciation of the environment. The argument that transport in itself damages the environment is beside the point. Like any other activity, transport should be subject to its true costs and benefits, including those inflicted on the environment. Simply freeing trade in commercial goods will not do either, since there are many instances in which it occurs at the expense of an undefended environment.

Creating the legal and institutional framework which is needed to take account of environmental effects requires international agreements. It is often difficult or impossible for individual countries to take any effective action with regard to common property issues. At the same time, international cooperation is aggravated by the gains that policy makers can appropriate at the expense of the environment (Andersson 1991b). Dealing with the situation will require that domestic and international measures are designed so as to pave the way for each other. The necessary components of a viable policy include property right reforms, pollution taxes and technological as well as financial transfers between countries.

Steps have now been taken by some countries, multilaterally or unilaterally, by firms, non-profit organizations and households to secure a sound environment. There are strongly differing views, however, about what action is needed. Many industrialized countries stress the importance of domestic policy reform in developing countries. Developing countries, on the other hand, emphasize the urgency of their other problems, and the much greater consumption of energy and natural resources in industrialized countries. The oil-producing countries refuse to consider any measures which would reduce the consumption of fossil fuels. Each country, or group of countries, looks to its own needs and interests, which produces a stalemate.

The new competition exerted by East Asia, and its influences on the world economy, affects the means and options to trade in this field as well. Let us briefly consider a number of arguments.

- Higher world incomes lead to a greater appreciation of the environment. Hence, the development of East Asia would stimulate goodwill, and attract qualified and harmonious workers or citizens.
- Technological progress provides opportunities for solutions to environmental problems. Japanese companies are among the leading proponents of 'green' technology, as seen in car emissions, among other things. Japan has announced that it will promote sustainable development worldwide.[8] MITI has opened a special environmental institute in Rite near Kyoto, the Research Institute of Innovative Technology for the Earth, with an annual budget of some US$60 million. Furthermore, Japanese companies are reported to view environmental considerations as less of a problem and more of an opportunity, compared with US firms. The attitudes of European firms lie in between. However, the Environment Agency in Tokyo is criticized for adopting a vague stance. Recommendations issued in the fall of 1992 called for firms to adopt a 'foreseeing' approach, which can hardly be interpreted in legal terms. Concerning corporate activities abroad, Japan asks private industry to make voluntary efforts.
- Industrialization in East Asia causes pollution which produces detrimental health effects. However, unless the environment is taken into account, prospects for development may suffer. When incomes rise, so do health requirements. In China, the speed of transformation has put great strain on ecosystems, both local and global.
- The limited endowments of natural resources in East Asia create a strong demand for imported commodities. Tropical forests, supplying inputs to the booming construction sector, are

located in relatively poor countries. Foreign firms may be granted temporary concessions to land, but not ownership. Hence, there is a lack of incentive to care for future production. The speed of deforestation in East Asia generally exceeds that in other developing countries. While burning by smallholders to clear land for agriculture is the major cause of deforestation elsewhere, industrial logging is the prime force in East Asia. The forests of the Philippines have already more or less disappeared, and exports have plummeted. In the eastern Malaysian state of Sarawak, where the indigenous peoples have resisted in vain, 500,000 hectares may now be logged annually according to Kumazaki (1992). Practically all virgin forest will then be gone by the mid-1990s. Thailand has legislated protection of the little it has left, but Thai firms are roaming the forests of Laos and Burma. Korean companies are starting to take on the huge Siberian forests, which used to be unreachable.

- Led by Malaysia, the resource-rich countries in Southeast Asia are vehemently opposed to any international settlement that would slow their exploitation of natural resources. At the same time, Malaysia is a strong antagonist of actions which would allow exploitation of common resources not located in national territories, such as those in the Antarctic or on the ocean floor.
- Economic pressures reduce the willingness of industrialized countries to provide compensation for non-commercial services. The United States in particular under the Reagan–Bush era refused to give up commercial gains for pollution control, or accept international transfer payments to deal with environmental issues. The West European countries, close to Chernobyl and other related catastrophes in Eastern Europe, are pressing for international solutions. At the same time, the EC is slow in dealing with waste control, and has been criticized for dumping waste in Eastern Europe and Africa.
- West European criticism of Southeast Asia's environmental record raises demands for trade barriers to enforce change. The EC, on the other hand, is accused of using environmental concerns as a scapegoat to avoid speaking about its already protectionist policies, e.g. in agriculture and textiles. By depriving developing countries of huge export incomes, these worsen their ability to deal with the environment.
- Ancient attitudes and customs often account for a strong demand for 'exotic' species, the rarer the better. In East Asia there is still

a lack of any countervailing environmental awareness among the general public. The availability of spending money, coupled with the beliefs of gentlemen concerned with dwindling sexual prowess, has made the horn of the rhino or the bone of the Bengal tiger rank among the most valuable substances on earth. The Coelacanth fish, close relative to the ancestor of all reptiles, birds and mammals, may have to end its some 400 million years on earth for the same reason (*Science & Vie* 1992). If such sentiments are to predominate, myth and nimbus lead to the death of species, not their survival.

Economic developments in East Asia, and the responses they trigger, exert ambiguous influences on the options for functioning 'trade' in non-commercial services. Higher incomes, greater awareness of environmental values and technological progress facilitate market and policy solutions. At the same time, there is a squandering of resources, and defensive reactions. As mismanagement of the environment continues, the lack of mechanisms with which to remedy the situation increases the pressure on the multilateral trade system.

5

THE THIRD LEG OF THE TRIANGLE

We have noted the argument that a liberal world order would require the leadership of a single hegemonic power, such as Great Britain in the nineteenth century and the United States throughout most of the twentieth century. Owing to its domestic problems as well as the rise of new centres of gravity, the United States is unlikely to resume a major responsibility for an open world economy. The attitudes in different regions will continue to have mutual repercussions. The stance adopted by Western Europe, particularly the EC, will strongly influence to what extent the United States will move towards sophisticated and deliberate protectionism, or whether the tide will turn.

In both Europe and East Asia, there is a marked tendency towards regionalization of economic transactions. At the same time, relations are severely underdeveloped between these two parts of the world. This chapter focuses on the changing conditions in Western Europe, and the implications of the weak European link with East Asia. Initially, the discussion is based on trade and investment data regarding the exchange between these two regions. The rest of the chapter is concerned with the European integration process and its impact on Europe itself as well as on its external relations – with particular emphasis on East Asian firms and countries.

5.1 A TRIANGLE OF ECONOMIC RELATIONS

The bulk of world trade in goods and factors is nowadays characterized by a triangle. The nodes correspond to North America, Western Europe and East Asia. Broadly speaking, the flows of trade and investment along the three sides display the following patterns.

- Between North America and Western Europe, there are intense relations. These are fairly balanced.
- The North American–East Asian side of the triangle also exhibits highly developed interactions, even though the volumes of exports and investments towards North America far exceed the corresponding flows in the opposite direction.
- The relations between East Asia and Western Europe are relatively undeveloped, especially as regards trade and investment towards East Asia.

These arguments follow from any measurement of the intensity of the flows between the three corners of the triangle. Because of their weights in the respective regions, the focus here is on the United States, the EC and Japan. For studying US export penetration of

Table 5.1 Export intensities, i.e. exports of the United States, European Community and Japan to a number of East Asian countries and country groups in per thousand of GDP of the United States, European Community and Japan respectively

Country	1970	1980	1990
Japan			
United States	4.6	7.7	8.8
EC	2.1	2.1	4.8
South Korea			
United States	0.6	1.7	2.6
EC	0.2	0.4	1.2
Japan	4.0	5.1	6.0
Taiwan			
United States	0.4	1.7	2.1
EC	0.2	0.5	1.0
Japan	3.2	5.0	5.3
ANIEs			
United States	1.6	5.6	7.4
EC	1.7	2.7	4.8
Japan	12.6	18.4	19.3
Thailand			
United States	0.2	0.5	0.5
EC	0.4	0.3	0.7
Japan	2.2	1.8	3.1
ASEAN			
US	1.1	3.4	3.4
EC	1.9	2.4	3.4
Japan	8.9	12.4	11.3

Sources: International Monetary Fund 1992; International Monetary Fund, *Directory of Trade Statistics*, various issues

Japan, US exports to Japan are either compared with US exports to the EC or with EC exports to Japan. Because flows from different regions to one and the same market are considered, the disputed degree of Japanese 'openness' can be compensated.

In order to be able to draw comparisons between figures from different countries, Table 5.1 eliminates the variation in size between markets by dividing export figures by GDP in the exporting country. Thus, intra-regional trade does not affect the analysis. In Table 5.2, on the other hand, exports are divided by the total exports of the exporting country. In this case, intra-EC trade is excluded in order to facilitate a comparison between the United States and the EC. In Table 5.3, the exercise is repeated for manufactured exports to Japan. Table 5.4, finally, calculates imports

Table 5.2 Export intensities, i.e. exports of the United States, European Community and Japan to a number of East Asian countries and country groups as a percentage of total exports of the United States, European Community and Japan respectively

Country	1970	1980	1990
Japan			
United States	10.76	9.42	12.36
EC	3.47	2.87	5.10
South Korea			
United States	1.47	2.12	3.66
EC	0.38	0.58	1.33
Japan	4.23	4.13	6.08
Taiwan			
United States	0.84	2.11	2.94
EC	0.31	0.69	1.09
Japan	3.39	4.09	5.37
ANIEs			
United States	3.81	6.82	10.38
EC	2.79	3.62	5.16
Japan	13.29	14.90	19.75
Thailand			
United States	0.35	0.57	0.76
EC	0.61	0.44	0.78
Japan	2.32	1.48	3.18
ASEAN			
United States	2.54	4.15	4.82
EC	3.13	3.24	3.60
Japan	9.36	10.03	11.49

Sources: See Table 5.1
Note: For the EC, intra-EC trade is excluded from total trade.

Table 5.3 Exports of manufactures of the United States and the European Community to Japan as a percentage of GDP, total exports, total exports of manufactures, total exports to Japan

	1970	*1980*	*1990*
United States			
Share of GDP	0.193	0.320	0.400
Share of total exports	4.5	3.9	5.6
Share of total exports of manufactures	6.6	6.0	9.2
Share of total exports to Japan	42	42	45
EC			
Share of GDP	0.186	0.184	0.360
Share of total exports (incl. internal trade)	1.00	0.77	1.57
Share of total exports (excl. internal trade)	n.a.	1.8	3.9
Share of total exports of manufactures (incl. internal trade)	1.3	1.1	2.0
Share of total exports of manufactures (excl. internal trade)	2.6	2.1	5.3
Share of total exports to Japan	87	84	75

Sources: See Table 5.1
Note: For the EC, intra-EC trade is excluded when noted.

from East Asian countries divided by the GDP of the importing country.

Throughout, the United States has had a considerably higher export intensity than the EC with regard to Japan. The gap was particularly large around 1980. The corresponding figures for South Korea, Taiwan or the ANIEs as a group display a similar pattern. The United States was ahead, although the EC caught up somewhat between 1980 and 1990. Relative to GDP, the EC's export intensity to Japan and South Korea more than doubled in the 1980s. The United States continued to raise the intensity of its exports to the region in the 1980s, but at a slower pace compared with the previous decade. The United States and the EC had about the same emphasis on exports to ASEAN, however.

Japan had a relatively large export intensity with respect to both the ANIEs and ASEAN. In the ANIEs, Japan's export intensity was two and a half times higher than that of the United States, and

Table 5.4 Import intensities, i.e. imports from East Asian countries into the United States, European Community and Japan as per thousand of GNP of the importing country

Country	1970	1980	1990
Japan			
United States	6.2	12.3	16.9
EC	3.0	6.3	10.1
South Korea			
United States	0.4	1.7	3.5
EC	0.1	0.9	1.4
Japan	1.1	2.9	4.0
Taiwan			
United States	0.6	2.5	4.3
EC	0.2	0.9	2.0
Japan	1.1	2.0	2.9
ANIEs			
United States	2.0	6.8	11.5
EC	1.4	4.2	6.1
Japan	3.1	6.9	8.8
Thailand			
United States	0.1	0.3	1.0
EC	0.2	0.6	0.8
Japan	0.9	1.1	1.4
ASEAN			
United States	1.0	4.8	5.2
EC	1.6	3.0	3.7
Japan	9.1	20.1	9.9

Sources: See Table 5.1

four times higher than that of the EC. In ASEAN, it was more than three times as high. The general pattern in the weight of exports is unchanged when they are divided by total exports instead of GDP. Table 5.2 indicates that Japanese exports have remained much more focused on East Asia than those from Western economies. The United States in particular has partly caught up in the ANIEs, however, while Japan has retained a substantial lead in ASEAN, which received 11.5 per cent of its total exports in 1990.

Furthermore, an examination of the distribution of exports tends to magnify the US emphasis on East Asia relative to that of the EC. It should be noted that this impression would be even stronger if intra-EC exports, boosted by price differentiation between the segmented European markets, had not been excluded. While the United States exported above 12 per cent of total exports to Japan in 1990, the corresponding figure for the EC was only some 5 per cent. In the ANIEs, the United States retained an export intensity which is about twice as high as that of the EC. At the same time, both of the Western regions strongly raised the share of their respective total exports going to these countries. In ASEAN, the United States was only marginally ahead of the EC.

The EC has performed somewhat better in manufactured exports. Still, Table 5.3 conveys the message of a weaker record for the EC in Japan compared with the United States in this case as well. As can be seen at the bottom of the table, more than 80 per cent of the EC's exports to Japan in 1970 and 1980 consisted of manufactures. By 1990 the share had fallen to 75 per cent. For the United States, manufactures accounted for only 45 per cent of total exports to Japan. In 1990, the intensity of the EC's manufactured exports to Japan relative to GDP was not far behind that of the United States, which represented a considerable catching up compared with the situation ten years earlier. As a share of total external exports, however, the EC manufactured exports to Japan amounted to 1.8 per cent in 1980, and 3.9 per cent in 1990. For the United States, the corresponding figures were 3.9 and 5.6 per cent.

Compared with the distribution of total manufactured exports, the EC is further behind the United States in Japan. Excluding EC's internal trade, the EC exported 2.1 per cent of its total manufactured exports to Japan in 1980. The share grew to 5.3 per cent in 1990. As will be further discussed later, however, the nature of this increase is questionable. Anyway, the corresponding figures for the United States were 6 per cent in 1980 and 9.2 per cent in 1990. Thus, even in the case of manufactures there were relatively lower levels of exports to Japan from the EC than from the United States, compared with the record of the respective regions in other markets.

Turning to import intensities, Table 5.4 shows a consistently greater emphasis on East Asia for the United States compared with the EC. In 1970 and 1980, Japan accounted for about twice as much of US imports. By 1990, the discrepancy had diminished in relative terms, as the EC imported 10 per cent and the United States 17 per cent from Japan. In the case of the ANIEs, the gap instead widened in the 1980s. In 1990, the United States imported 11.5 per cent of its total imports from these countries, while the corresponding figure for the EC was 6.1 per cent. In the case of ASEAN, there was less of a difference. Meanwhile, Japan imported a smaller share of its total imports from the ANIEs than the United States did. The share of imports coming from ASEAN was almost twice as large in Japan as in the United States, and even greater relative to that of the EC. This reflects the larger imports of raw materials from ASEAN, while it has taken time for the ANIEs to succeed in raising their manufactured exports to Japan.

Finally, comparing the stocks of direct investment, Tables 5.5 and 5.6 indicate a highly skewed pattern. According to home country data, West Germany held twenty times as much investment in the United States as in Japan in 1985, and the UK forty times as much in 1984. The stock of Japanese direct investment in the United States was about 2.5 times as large as that in Western Europe in the mid-1980s. According to the data reported by host countries, Japan attracted almost three times as much direct investment from the United States as from Western Europe in 1971, and twice as much as of 1986. The United States provided 51.7 per cent of the cumulative flow of direct investment to Japan during the period 1951–89, while the total share of Western Europe was 23.2 per cent (Ministry of Finance 1991).

To sum up, the comparisons of export and import intensities and the pattern of direct investments point to an imbalanced triangular

Table 5.5 Stock of foreign direct investment in Japan and the United States, as reported by the home country (million US$)

Country	1971	1981	1983	1984	1986
United States					
in Japan	1,821	6,762	7,661	7,936	11,333
in Western Europe	n.a.	n.a.	n.a.	n.a.	n.a.
West Germany					
in Japan	n.a.	573	685	687	736[a]
in United States	n.a.	11,380	13,671	15,385	15,217[a]
The Netherlands					
in Japan	n.a.	n.a.	n.a.	339	n.a.
in United States	n.a.	8,633	11,702	13,815	n.a.
UK					
in Japan	39	380	n.a.	841	n.a.
in United States	1,935	16,181	n.a.	35,179	n.a.
Japan					
in United States	918	11,341	16,675	20,035	35,596
in Western Europe	725	5,076	6,942	8,878	14,277

Sources: International Monetary Fund 1989; UNCTC 1988
Notes: [a] 1985.
       n.a., not available.

Table 5.6 Stock of foreign direct investment in the United States, West Germany, the UK, Thailand and Japan as reported by the host country (million US$)

Country	1971	1981	1983	1984	1986
United States					
from Western Europe	10,337	72,264	92,874	108,115	141,547
from Japan	–227	7,697	11,336	16,044	23,433
West Germany					
from Western Europe	n.a.	16,224	15,178	14,566	14,647[a]
from United States	n.a.	13,581	13,333	11,895	11,578[a]
from Japan	n.a.	1,276	1,368	1,521	1,797[a]
UK					
from Western Europe	3,521	13,345	n.a.	4,871	n.a.
from United States	1,935	16,181	n.a.	35,179	n.a.
from Japan	39	380	n.a.	841	n.a.
Japan					
from Western Europe	151	842	1,039	1,180	1,637
from United States	572	1,761	2,441	2,655	3,407
	1970	*1975*	*1980*	*1987*	
Thailand					
from EC	4.0	64.0	157.0	383.0	
from Sweden	0.2	0.9	1.3	10.7	
from United States	17.0	202.0	324.0	792.0	
from Japan	16.0	138.0	287.0	824.0	

Sources: International Monetary Fund 1989; UNCTC 1988; data printouts obtained from the Economic and Social Commission for Asia and the Pacific
Notes: [a] 1985.
      n.a., not available.

flow in world trade and investments. The European–East Asian side is the least developed. European progress regarding its exports of manufactured goods to Japan demonstrates that success is possible. In terms of its overall manufactured exports, however, the EC still sells a smaller share in Japan than the United States does. There was an even more limited amount of EC direct investment in Japan compared with that of the United States. The discrepancy is equally pronounced with respect to the ANIEs, while the United States and the EC have a more equal exchange with ASEAN.

5.2 THE IMBALANCES – MISSED OPPORTUNITIES AND LOOMING RISKS

The economic relations between Western Europe and East Asia are not only under-exploited, they are also severely imbalanced.

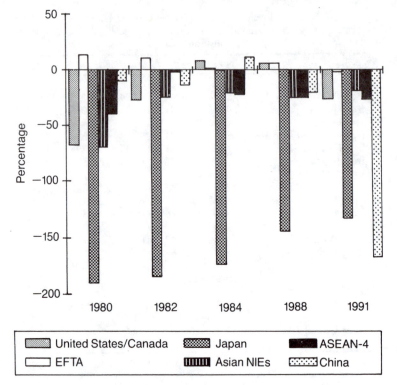

Figure 5.1 The EC's external trade balances as a percentage of exports to regions
Source: Eurostat 1984, 1987, 1989, 1992

Although there is nothing strange or bad about bilateral imbalances in trade *per se*, it is still interesting to consider how the actual interactions between different trading partners develop over time. Most trade is now of the intra-industry kind, and is determined by the handling of technology, information and human skills rather than, for example, differences between countries in factor endowments. The direction of trade flows indicates, among other things, which way countries orient their efforts and where they collect information.

Figures 5.1 and 5.2 depict the EC's trade balance with external countries as a percentage of its exports to those countries and of the EC's total external exports, respectively. The EC had a deficit with North America in 1980, which was converted into a surplus in 1984

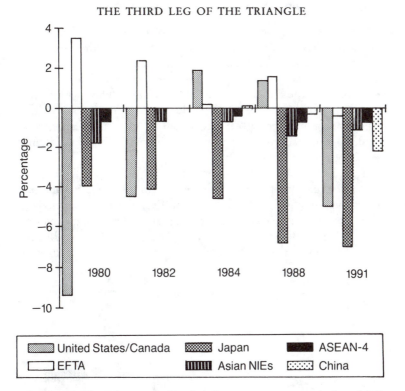

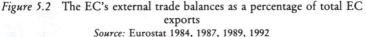

Figure 5.2 The EC's external trade balances as a percentage of total EC
exports
Source: Eurostat 1984, 1987, 1989, 1992

and 1988 in the wake of the strong dollar. By 1991, the balance had
been turned around again. As Figure 5.2 indicates, the United States
at present accounts for the second largest of the EC's deficits with
any trading partners, although the gap is modest relative to the total
trade with the United States. With EFTA, the EC has had a slight
trade surplus, mostly between 0 and 2 per cent of total exports.
With Japan and the other export-oriented economies in East Asia,
on the other hand, the EC has had a consistent trade deficit.

In relation to the EC's exports to respective country/region,
Figure 5.1 shows that the deficit with Japan shrank from nearly 200
per cent in 1980 to less than 150 per cent in 1991. Compared with
the total exports of the EC, however, Figure 5.2 shows that this
deficit increased from about 4 per cent in 1980 to about 7 per cent
in 1988 and 1991. There has also been an uninterrupted deficit in

the trade with both the ANIEs and ASEAN (excluding Singapore). The former has corresponded to about 2 per cent of the EC's total exports, and the latter about 1.5 percentage points. Meanwhile, trade with China has developed quite spectacularly in the last few years. In 1991, the EC experienced an even larger deficit with China than with Japan in terms of the volume of exports going to the respective country. To a great extent, China's exports emanate from off-shore production by firms which originate in East Asia, and especially the ANIEs.

In the EC's trade with various regions of developing countries, Asia has taken over the predominant position. Figures 5.3 and 5.4 depict the composition of trade for the EC, in this case excluding Spain, Portugal and Greece, with five regions of developing countries in 1970, 1980 and 1990 respectively. From a fairly even distribution of the EC's exports in 1970, Africa and the Middle East gained in

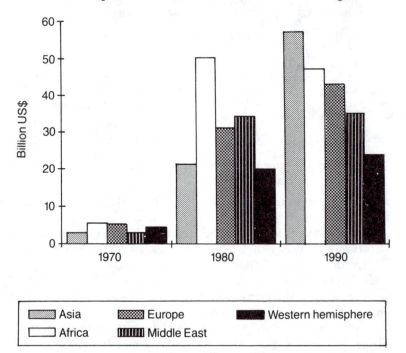

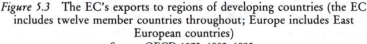

Figure 5.3 The EC's exports to regions of developing countries (the EC includes twelve member countries throughout; Europe includes East European countries)
Source: OECD 1972, 1982, 1992a

importance up to 1980, Asia retained its position, while Europe (i.e. Eastern Europe) and the Western hemisphere accounted for declining shares. By 1990, however, Asia had become the dominant destination among developing countries, while Africa and the Middle East in particular had stagnated. The EC's imports show a similar pattern. Of the other developing countries, only those in Europe recorded any tangible increase in the 1980s. As expected, the share of the Middle East contracted dramatically, in line with falling oil prices, African exports stagnated and those from the Western hemisphere increased only marginally.

East Asian dynamism has resulted in large surpluses in its bilateral trade with the EC, while returns on European financial investments have provided some compensation. The volume of trade has grown in both directions, although the imbalances have

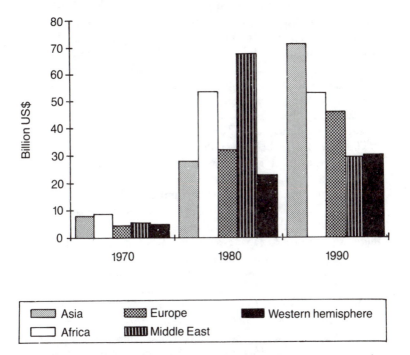

Figure 5.4 The EC's imports from regions of developing countries (the EC includes twelve member countries throughout; Europe includes East European countries)
Source: OECD 1972, 1982, 1992a

widened compared with the EC's total trade. This is not least due to the increased attention paid by East Asian firms to Europe in the late 1980s. To provide some anecdotal evidence from that time, *Newsweek* (1989) reported standing room only at seminars in Japan focusing on the EC market. Sumitomo Bank was said to devote as much attention to Europe as to the United States. Sony Corporation, according to the same article, had appointed its senior European manager to its board of directors.

As far as trade with the United States is concerned, the imbalances reflect severe macroeconomic problems. Appropriate policy adjustments, or additional protectionist measures, will eventually reduce US imports and investment from East Asia. As the EC's propensity to import from East Asia remains relatively low, there is still a great potential for raising it. Moreover, corrections by the United States may further intensify East Asian efforts to sell in Europe. The nature of European exports to Japan in particular also raises certain questions. In the late 1980s, the EC's exports to Japan grew strongly, with a bias towards luxury products in the form of cosmetics, design, alcoholic beverages and grandiose motor vehicles. Such products, which accounted for about half of the increase in the EC's exports to Japan between 1987 and 1990, have fared badly as a result of the lower Japanese growth of recent years. It is questionable whether they form the basis for a healthier trade balance in the future.

The prevailing imbalances indicate missed opportunities, particularly on the part of Europeans in East Asia. First, the relatively larger US export and import intensities across the Pacific might suggest that there are missed opportunities on behalf of the EC in East Asia. Second, higher export and investment intensities across the Atlantic than those Japan has achieved with the EC indicate that there are still missed Japanese opportunities in Europe. Third, the greater export and investment figures accounted for by the Japanese in both the United States and the EC suggest missed opportunities in East Asia on behalf of both these regions.

Moreover, US exports to Japan and the ANIEs, as well as the size of American investments there, outperform those achieved by Europe. This is despite the fundamental imbalances in the US macroeconomy. While Europeans have supposedly more internationally oriented companies and management than the Americans, who were for a long time able to rely on their large domestic market, US firms have been more active in East Asia. The weakness of the EC's record also stands out from a comparison of investments undertaken by EC firms and Swiss firms in Japan. The Swiss economy is admittedly sophisticated, and well known for high-quality products. Nevertheless, it may appear somewhat surprising that a country with only 3 per cent of the GDP of OECD Europe is the largest investor in Japan, accounting for 37 per cent of the total European flow to that country between 1951 and 1989 (Ministry of Finance 1991).

The impression of missed European opportunities is underscored by the concerns in smaller East Asian countries of becoming dominated by other actors. This may be associated with the economic weight of Japan, the political clout of America or the future ambitions of China. Such sentiments do create an outright demand for expanded relations with European firms and countries, e.g. in ASEAN. These countries have special programmes to attract European investment.

The persistent imbalance in the European–East Asian trade gives rise to friction. Again, there may be nothing wrong or abnormal about bilateral deficits. In the present context, however, the imbalance is connected with a general lack of knowledge in Europe. Asians have recently become much more active in exploiting the missing link between the regions, but few Europeans put a priority on expanding exports and investment activities in East Asia.

5.3 STAGES OF EUROPEAN INTEGRATION

From 1973 onwards, the economic record of the EC deteriorated in absolute as well as relative terms. As can be seen from Table 5.7, the EC countries accounted for some 4–5 per cent of annual growth in the earlier periods. Between 1973 and 1979, average annual growth was about 2–3 per cent, while the UK lagged behind. In 1979–85, growth rates declined to approximately 1 per cent. The record in terms of industrial growth was even poorer, although the UK recovered somewhat in this respect. Japan and the United States also experienced lower growth rates than previously, but performed better than the EC.

Slow growth coupled with problems of inflation and unemployment made Eurosclerosis a label for the stagnant conditions of an old and 'tired' continent. In the research project 'Costs of non-Europe', the EC Commission partly blamed the limited economic integration between the member countries. European firms tend to

Table 5.7 Growth rates in European countries

Country	Average annual growth rate (%)					
	GDP				Industry	
	1960–8	1968–73	1973–9	1979–85	1965–80	1980–6
Germany, Federal Republic	4.0	4.9	2.3	1.3	2.9	0.7
France	5.4	5.4	2.8	1.1	4.6	0.6
The Netherlands	4.8	4.9	2.7	0.7	3.6	0.5
Belgium	4.5	5.6	2.2	1.2	4.4	0.5
UK	3.0	3.4	1.5	1.2	1.2	2.0
Italy	5.7	4.5	3.7	1.4	4.2	0.2
United States	4.5	3.2	2.4	2.5	1.9	3.2
Japan	10.2	8.6	3.6	4.0	8.5	5.0
Sweden	4.4	3.7	1.8	1.8	2.2	2.5

Sources: OECD 1987, 1992b

be too small to exploit advantages of scale fully, rendering an inefficient resource utilization, while they are too large for their domestic markets, resulting in monopolistic pricing. Such problems, as well as the growing pressure to handle the new competition from Japan and the ANIEs, gradually intensified the quest for European integration. Broadly speaking, the process has followed three stages.

1 The first period was driven primarily by visions. The Treaty of Rome was signed and great plans were formulated to prevent future wars between France and Germany. A new Europe was to be constructed in order to match the United States and the Soviet Union, both of which were viewed as formidable competitors at the time. By creating a stronger Europe, it was hoped that electorates would not choose to sacrifice political and economic freedoms for higher growth.

2 The second phase was initiated as these pressures from outside disappeared. The political goal to establish a close relationship between France and Germany seemed to have been reached. It no longer appeared impossible to compete with the Americans and most people forgot that there had ever been any competitive threat from the economy of the Soviet Union. The major feature of the EC became a growing bureaucracy rather than further liberalization. Brussels regulated production and trade in agriculture, as well as production in industries such as steel, ship-building

and textiles. The ideals had lost their power. Europessimism grew.

3 The third stage was the Renaissance. New pressures have evolved, this time in the form of competition from Japan and East Asia. The creation of the Single Market, initiated in the mid-1980s and finalized at the end of 1992, has led the way.

The programme for establishing a Single Market was set out in the 1985 White Paper 'Completing the Internal Market'. Its message was reinforced in mid-1987 by the passing of the Single European Act, which instituted a weighted form of majority voting as the norm in the Council of Ministers for the passing of the 1992 directive. This amounted to a binding commitment to fulfil the internal market. Although most of the originally planned steps were on schedule for settlement at the end of 1992, crucial issues which will influence the final outcome still remain.

Achieving a borderless European market in such a short time has been an extremely ambitious project. However, not even the 1992 programme turned out to be sufficient to deal with the new demands. The West European outsiders in EFTA, already strongly integrated with the EC in economic terms, became enchanted by the momentum of the Single Market and concerned about the risk of discrimination. In the late 1980s, this contributed to a major expansion of direct investment in the EC from these countries, particularly Sweden. After several years of negotiations, the European Economic Area (EEA) has opened the door to a factual expansion of the four freedoms to the EFTA countries as well. Border controls will remain, however, since the EEA is not a customs union.

To join the EEA, the EFTA countries have to comply with most of the decisions already taken by the EC authorities. The EC has not cast any doubts upon its institutional system, and the autonomy of its decision making. To attain full liberalization with regard to the Single Market, and in order to influence its future course rather than merely implement decisions already taken by the EC, it is necessary to attain full membership in the Community. Several of the original EFTA countries have joined the EC over the years, and the model of shunning supra-national coordination and bureaucracy appears to have lost ground, at least among policy makers. Austria, Sweden, Finland and perhaps other countries in Western Europe now opt for membership in the EC. Many Eastern European countries would certainly wish to join as well, but can only hope for certain favours from their integrating Western neighbours for the time being.

However, the changing circumstances both outside and within the EC have raised additional demands. The breakdown of the formerly planned economies in Eastern Europe has opened up new opportunities for peace and political freedom. On the other hand, the breakdown of the established power structures, along with the deplorable conditions in Eastern Europe, has created an unpredictable situation. Several national states born out of the turbulence in Europe at the end of the Second World War have rapidly disintegrated. The tensions within the former Yugoslavia have escalated into outright war and tremendous suffering for the civilian population. The USSR has split up, and not even Russia can be certain about keeping its territory intact in the future.

The external events contributed to the perception that, in order to become an energetic player in this new world, the EC had to form a political union as well. Such plans appeared already in the early 1970s, but the tide of the continuing integration within the Community now moved with much greater weight in that direction. The expanding transactions across the borders accounted for rising costs of conversion between the national currencies and prospects of growing monetary instability. To complete a single market for capital and forgo the risk of inconsistent national policies, it was felt that 'fixed' exchange rates were not enough. The need to achieve a tight coordination of monetary and economic policy objectives in general contributed to concrete plans for a political as well as a monetary union, and a common central bank (Committee for the Study of Economic and Monetary Union 1989).

The political handling of these demands has been highly effective, partly as a result of the momentum built up by the 1992 programme, and partly because the member countries risked running into great trouble unless they went ahead. This resulted in the pathbreaking Maastricht Summit in December 1991, at which the EC decided to form the European Union (EU). The treaty was signed in February 1992. Confronted with direct questions of whether to ratify it, however, the European peoples have turned out to be strongly divided. The outcome of the referendum in Denmark called the whole process of European integration into question. Although other member countries have responded more favourably and the acute crisis seems to have been overcome, suspicion continues to flourish. Not only is the UK concerned with the prospects of losing sterling, but in many countries doubts are widely spread about assigning power to the unelected body of the European Commission. This has led to requests for a balance between the principle of subsidiarity, i.e. allowing each decision to be taken at a level as close as possible to the group affected by it, and the coordination of solutions to common problems at a supra-national level.

5.4 EFFECTS OF EUROPEAN INTEGRATION

So far, there have been many exceptions to free trade within the EC. This has been due to, for example, differing technical, hygienic and veterinary standards, and restrictions of the right to import services. The programme for establishing the Single Market at the end of 1992 stipulated that all interior barriers to trade were to disappear, public procurement was to be opened up and factor markets were to be deregulated. In addition, an increased budget has been agreed upon to support European R&D programmes and to enable a greater common responsibility for environmental, regional and social issues.

The countries in Western Europe are highly dependent on international trade. This applies particularly to the small industrialized nations such as Belgium, The Netherlands and the Scandinavian countries. As already discussed, most of the foreign trade occurs within the region and takes the form of intra-industry trade in differentiated manufactured products. There is relatively more inter-industry trade along the north–south dimension within the Community. Germany is generally the largest trading partner in both imports and exports. This applies to all the EC countries except Belgium – which has as much trade with France as with Germany – and those at the periphery, i.e. Ireland, Greece and Portugal.

Given the dominance of intra-industry trade, the primary effect of the 1992 programme is higher efficiency due to intensified competition and, to a lesser extent, scale economies. A company located in one member country becomes able to operate more effectively in the others. Meanwhile, competition will increase in its own territory. Simulation models have predicted that prices will decline and production increase in industries characterized by imperfect competition and scale advantages. Smith and Venables (1988) prophesied reduced corporate profits and the forced exit of many firms from the market. Another probable implication is less intra-industry trade as price discrimination ceases, and consequently less intra-European trade as a whole.[1] Of course, sectors are affected differently because of varying costs for transport and communication, and because the original level of competition differed. Welfare effects of structural adjustment caused by the attraction of resources from one industry to another are more complex and require careful study.[2]

In its valuations of the 1992 programme, the EC Commission expected a deflation of consumer prices by 6 per cent, a GDP 4 per cent higher, a strengthening of public finances by 2 per cent of GDP due to relaxed budgetary and external constraints, 1.8 million new jobs – reducing the jobless rate in Europe by 1.5 per cent – and, finally, an improvement of the external balance by 1 per cent of GDP. Given that governments were to give up some gains from fiscal consolidation and lower inflation, a 7 per cent increase in GDP and 5 million new employment opportunities were expected. In addition to these 'static' effects, others have argued for much larger 'dynamic' effects, for example due to more innovation as a consequence of intensified competition (Geroski 1988). Although the numerical estimates are extremely uncertain, there is little doubt that the dynamic effects will be the most important.

With integration between the member countries, one may expect a convergence in technology due to intensified competition as well as movements of factors of production. There is not yet much empirical evidence for this. In terms of prices, there were diverging disparities within the EC in the 1970s, and only a slight convergence in the 1980s (Emerson 1988). The relative income differences between the EC countries have diminished but the absolute differences continue to grow, which is what one would expect when comparing the growth of countries at dissimilar income levels.

Begg (1989) noted that various regions in the EC will be differently affected by integration depending on their degree of competitiveness. At the local level, there has clearly been a polarization between the urban areas which have benefited from European integration and those which have lost (Cheshire 1990). However, the effects vary across industries rather than across regions. The actual outcome of a particular location will hinge on the ability of its activities to take advantage of enhanced competition and improved opportunities for scale. This, in turn, will partly depend on its links with industries elsewhere, and the degree to which it can retain or attract favourable factors of production.

R&D belongs to those sectors which are expected to be the most influenced by the creation of the Single Market (Commission of the European Communities 1989). Here, a great potential for economies of scale prevails because of the harmonization of technical standards and greater competitive pressure. It should be noted, however, that economics a long time ago gave up trying to specify a relationship between market concentration and technological progress. Both are determined by other, more fundamental factors. Transforming modern technology into commercial production requires links which allow for mutual feedback of information. The EC lags behind in a number of high technology industries, and its position appears to have further weakened in the 1980s.

Even more than in the United States, R&D is undertaken by relatively small firms in Europe. Aware of the need to share efforts in order to catch up in high technology, private industry is engaged in an extensive restructuring. This includes vertical as well as horizontal integration through takeovers, mergers, technical alliances, etc. A number of large pan-European conglomerates have been formed after a wave of such actions. These often involve alliances between European and non-European companies, with both American and Japanese firms playing a major role. The fields of automobiles, telecommunications, mainframe computers and mini-computers provide many examples.

Apart from the initiatives by private industry, the Commission as well as the national governments in the Community support cooperative projects in R&D. Substantial programmes have been implemented which subsidize R&D on the basis that the output is shared, paving the way for joint ventures and other forms of corporate collaboration.[3] Some are financed by each firm's government, and require cooperation with firms from other countries. The virtues of such cooperation are far from clear, however, not least as agreements are open to strategic manipulation. Requirements to share the output of joint research programmes, for example, may reduce the incentive to develop new technology. An asymmetry in innovative ability may provide a similar disincentive. If subsidies make cooperation worthwhile anyway, there are likely to be losses for the side with the smaller ability to convert the output into commercial production. These issues will be returned to later.

Financial services represent another field subject to changing conditions as a result of integration. As is seen from Table 5.8, there are marked differences between the banking systems of the member countries in the Community. Each country has many banks, but the market share of the five largest tends to be substantial, with 50 per cent in France as the maximum. Moreover, there is a large variation between the individual countries in interest margins on demand and savings deposits, suggesting limited competition in price and more competition in offering convenient branch locations and other services (Neven 1990).

The second banking directive of 1989 accounted for freer competition and liberalization on a worldwide basis – although EC financial institutions must then be awarded the same access in the foreign markets.[4] This should inspire an intensified pursuit for innovative services. In most aspects of finance, however, customized relations and problems with monitoring represent substantial advantages for incumbents and barriers for outsiders. These complicate the options for acquisition and collaboration as well, and make it take time before major changes are borne out. Although a monetary union ought to make Europe more attractive, there will probably remain considerable impediments for foreign financial institutions (Feldman 1990; Shigehara 1990).

Because the member countries are heterogeneous in terms of, for example, culture, history, language and taste, there will be limitations on the degree of integration actually achieved in the EC. Above all, labour will remain quite immobile for many years to come. Further distortion in the allocation of resources will also follow from differences in the monetary and macroeconomic policies pursued by the member states, and even more so as long as they refrain from harmonizing tax rates.

At the same time, the dismantling of barriers and border controls make the member countries fiercer competitors *vis-à-vis* each other in the attraction of mobile factors of production. Such public competition within the EC will remove obstacles to efficiency and growth. On the other hand, there are also situations in which non-cooperative behaviour leads to sub-optimal outcomes. When that can be expected, it should be the task of the Commission to intervene and ensure a joint solution. Its limited ability to do so in practice is apparent from the policy inconsistencies which continue to prevail among the member countries. Thus, there is a need for the Commission to obtain increased legislative power. Again, however, such neutralization of public competition may prevent socially preferable outcomes, especially when joint solutions are motivated by the desire to defend vested interests.

Table 5.8 Comparison of selected banking systems, end 1986

	France	Germany, Federal Republic	Italy	UK	EC	United States	Japan
No. of foreign banks	131	148	38	300	889	459	54
No. of domestic banks	860	702	247	451	3,064	17,234	1,165
Assets of commercial banks (billion ECU)	947	425	497	969	3,835	2,732	2,616
Assets of other depository institutions (billion ECU)	329	585	159	194	1,457	1,234	2,125
Total assets/GDP	1.7	1.1	1.1	2.2	1.5	1.0	2.4
Market share of five largest banks (%)	50	16	30	36	13	10	20
Market share of foreign banks (%)[a]	16	4	3	60	–	–	3
International bank assets (billion US$)[b]	525	551	201	267	–	688	2,072

Sources: Shibuya 1990; Industrial Bank of Japan 1991
Notes: [a] End 1987;
[b] Outstanding 1990/9, except for Italy (end 1988).

The establishment of the EU should facilitate cooperative solutions in Europe, whether or not they are in the interest of the Community. This means that minorities which cannot have their way at the supra-national level will have to give in, which is partly the reason why the EU encounters opposition.[5] From the perspective of social welfare, it is crucial whether the Commission will handle the demands of interest groups better than the national governments do. As the distance grows between authorities and people, there may be increased disparities in the ability of groups to exert political pressure. The unlimited growth of lobbying activities around the bureaucrats in Brussels, not to speak of Strasbourg, represents a worrying development in this respect.

It can be concluded that the strengthening of the supra-national level accounts for a more effective handling of cross-border issues. Properly supplemented by the principle of subsidiarity, the outcome should be beneficial. If the system gets out of hand, or fails to free itself from vested interests, there may instead be increased mismanagement of political powers.

Beyond these developments, the establishment of a single European currency raises other intricate issues. This is due both to the difficulties of getting there in the first place and to doubts concerning the functioning of a common currency in itself. Before they are allowed to enter, the Maastricht Treaty requires the individual EC countries to achieve ambitious targets with respect to inflation, public finances in terms of government deficit as well as debt, exchange rate stability *vis-à-vis* the Exchange Rate Mechanism, and the long-term interest rate. At present, few countries fulfil these targets. Table 5.9 shows certain aspects of the European countries' economic record as predicted by OECD for 1992. Even in the 'hard core' of countries, the budget remains a problem. The same applies to the 'qualifiers'. These problems are even greater among the 'deviators', where inflation and the external balance also appear as troublesome areas. The level of unemployment is medium to high in practically all of Europe.

As was predicted, the integration of European markets, with the enormous expansion of financial transactions across national boundaries, has created monetary turbulence. This has been further magnified by the costs borne by Germany as a result of its assimilation of the former German Democratic Republic, and the ensuing demands on the monetary policy of that country compared with the rest of the Community. Not only did the British pound,

Table 5.9 Projected economic indicators in Europe for 1992

Countries	Inflation (% per year)	Budget (%/GDP)	External balance/GDP	Unemployment (% of working force)
'Hard core'				
Germany	3.5	−3.4	−0.8	4.7
Belgium	2.3	−5.5	2.6	9.7
The Netherlands	3.5	−3.4	−4.4	6.5
France	2.7	−2.3	−0.1	9.8
Denmark	2.1	−2.1	−2.3	10.7
'Qualifiers'				
Switzerland	3.6	–	4.0	2.5
Austria	3.8	−2.0	−0.4	4.0
Sweden	2.3	−4.1	−0.7	5.0
Norway	2.3	−2.9	−4.3	5.8
'Deviators'				
Great Britain	3.6	4.6	1.4	9.8
Italy	5.3	−11.3	−1.9	11.2
Finland	2.4	−7.7	−3.2	11.3
Spain	5.2	−4.9	−2.8	16.1
Ireland	2.8	−1.9	5.5	16.9
Greece	15.8	−14.5	−2.2	9.4
Portugal	9.5	–	−0.8	5.0

Source: OECD 1992c

but also the Italian lira and several other currencies drop out of the European exchange rate mechanism in the process. Europe has found itself in a position with overvalued exchange rates and a real rate of interest at a historically high level, accounting for extremely high capital costs and a short-term perspective in economic planning. Investments have crumbled, the external trade record has worsened and unemployment is soaring in most of Europe.

Whether a common currency can help is an open question. There is no doubt about the potential benefits of a monetary union. The excessive transaction costs between the European currencies would be eliminated, enabling savings and investments to meet throughout Europe with a considerably smaller efficiency loss on the way. However, the heterogeneous member countries will hardly have even a remote resemblance to an 'optimal currency area' within the foreseeable future. In addition to the low mobility of labour, there is considerable wage and price stickiness, and a lack of mechanisms to transfer funds on a scale sufficient to counterweigh external shocks that hit the member countries asymmetrically. Appropriate instruments for adjustment would require a much expanded budget for the central authorities.

Finally, there may be incentive problems in the formulation of budgetary policies in the individual member countries of the EU. It is still far from clear what objectives a central bank would have, and how it could secure an optimal monetary policy and budget discipline. Although the national budgets are to be regulated in the EU, authorities may find ways to attract factors of production through reduced taxes and increased expenditures on infrastructure, if not outright subsidies, while spreading the costs across the Community as a whole.[6] If only a few countries 'managed' to behave in such a way, a monetary union would become destabilizing and, in fact, produce intolerable results. Preventing such behaviour is likely to restrict the room for subsidiarity, taking us back to the political complications.

5.5 EFFECTS ON THE REST OF THE WORLD

Apart from the domestic issues, Europe must formulate its relations with the rest of the world. Practically all calculations of the welfare effects of 1992 on the Community itself have assumed that the level of external barriers is to be left essentially unchanged. So far, the EC has served as a customs union with a common external tariff, but with no other clear definition of common rules for external policy. In particular, the members have maintained different quantitative restrictions on imports from third countries, which cannot continue in the Single Market. It is far from straightforward how to convert twelve external policies into a single 'unchanged' one. In practice, there will be either an 'opening' or a 'closing' with respect to external flows of trade and investment. The EC's behaviour *vis-à-vis* the rest of the world, as well as the responses triggered from outside, will strongly influence the final outcome of the whole integration process.

Let us consider how the rest of the world will be affected by the European integration. The deregulation of the Single Market should be helpful for Europe's own economic development. Further gains will be achieved through a functioning EEA. In both cases, the positive effects will grow out of the removal of West European DTBs. East European reforms in the same direction should eventually provide benefits to all of Europe. The restructuring within Europe reduces trade obstacles for outsiders too. The reduction in DTBs provides economies of scale to Japanese and other East Asian firms as well as to other outsiders that approach European markets, unless discriminated against in some way, of course.

Given an improved utilization of resources and higher incomes in the EC, other countries will benefit from a general trade creation. This will be particularly strong if the EC achieves permanently higher growth. The effects should be felt the most in EC imports of income-sensitive goods and services. In addition, the nature of the trade-creating effect will depend on the direction of the shift in competitiveness within the Community. An improved investment and savings efficiency should lead to greater access to capital relative to labour and natural resources, which will presumably support comparative advantages in capital-intensive manufacturing and services.

Economic development will also depend on the organization of business operations, and how technology and information are handled. The inflow of direct investment will play a significant role in this context. Investments undertaken by firms from the relatively technology- and capital-intensive EFTA countries, and the possible inclusion of EFTA itself in the Community, create a further potential for movements in this direction. The same applies to investments by US and Japanese firms, of which the latter will be more thoroughly discussed below. However, any shift is slowed unless restructuring is allowed. The EC must not apply quotas and subsidies against outsiders to maintain shrinking activities. In addition, a competitive pressure will not suffice in the absence of linkages which allow knowledge to be converted into commercial products.

Given that the EC's comparative advantage tilts towards capital intensity, and new technologies are successfully managed, the EC should become a more formidable competitor with other industrialized countries. The large investments in the Community will initially make capital more scarce worldwide and will lead to a universal increase in interest rates. More efficient capital markets in the EC would partly offset this effect, however. There would also be a potential for expanded inter-industry trade, to the benefit of developing countries. On the other hand, these export mainly low-elasticity products to the EC, which at present represents only a small share of their market (Page 1991).

Developments in Eastern Europe, and their relationship to Western Europe, add further complications. The assimilation of

Eastern Germany has already made capital notably more costly in Europe. To the extent that Eastern Europe gains preferential access to the markets in Western Europe, those countries would attract some of the investments otherwise directed towards the Community. In the absence of successful industrialization in Eastern Europe, on the other hand, there will be great pressure for labour migration to the Community. If this takes place on a large scale (although it seems politically and socially inconceivable at the present time), the EC's comparative advantage would change towards lower labour costs. The same would occur if countries in Eastern Europe became new members of the Community.

In addition to trade-creating effects, there will also be trade diversion, meaning that exports are shifted from current outside trading partners to less efficient partners within the Community. The developing countries, for example, already experience this effect in standardized products, which have low value added and are highly price elastic. The trade diversion will be stronger the more southern Europe specializes in the production of such goods. With further preferential access for Eastern Europe, there will be even greater trade diversion in that direction.

A number of studies have calculated outcomes for various external regions under different circumstances. According to Han (1992), the exports of the ANIEs, e.g. in electrical goods and office machinery, will be more adversely affected by European integration than those from other developing countries, the prime reason being that such items should be subject to particularly large productivity increases within the Community. From the macroeconomic perspective, the trade-creating effects are likely to outweigh the negative price effects. Again, however, the trade diversion may be amplified by increased inter-country specialization within the Community and the attraction of direct investment.

5.6 EUROPEAN COMMUNITY PROTECTIONISM

The most crucial determinant of trade diversion is the Community's external policy. The Commission has given assurances that the average level of protection will not increase. This stance is supported by the EC's vested interests in trade. Its external exports amount to 20 per cent of world exports, and 9 per cent of the EC's own GDP. It may be argued that the EC as a whole is 'unlikely to shift to a systematically more protectionist stance. Such a shift would require greater similarity among member states' levels of competitiveness and attitudes.'[7]

Nevertheless, a common external trade policy is still lacking. It has not been shown how the national quotas on textiles allowed under the Multifiber Arrangement will be shared, and the expensive agricultural policy still remains a source of distress, not only burdening European taxpayers and natural exporters of food products around the world, but hurting the multilateral trade system as a whole. In fact, current policies do not lend much support to the official position of the Commission. A number of studies have concluded that the EC antidumping law progressively gives rise to trade measures which are inconsistent with GATT, and have a severe negative impact.

The background to the antidumping policy is the difficulty of obtaining community-wide VERs, as approval of the Council of Ministers is normally blocked by Germany, Britain and The Netherlands. In the Tokyo Round, the EC pushed for an amendment of Article XIX of the GATT to allow for selective action against 'disruptive imports', i.e. imports from new suppliers. Although the EC set this against acceptance of the Tokyo Round as a whole, the threat was not pursued in the end. Rather, the antidumping weapon has enabled the Commission to acquire what it did not get at that time.

In contrast with Article XIX, which does not allow discrimination, antidumping proceedings deal with specific companies. Given the calculation principles, Hindley (1988) and Palmeter (1989) showed that practically any exporter can be found guilty of dumping. Arguments that the targeted firms would be based in countries which use discriminatory trade policies themselves totally lack credibility, as can be seen from the cases made against Hong Kong. Instead, Messerlin (1989) demonstrated a connection between antidumping and the ability of local industry to exert political pressure. The reason for actually implemented cases is rather the absence of a readiness to agree to VERs. As discussed in Chapter 4, the seriousness of the policy cannot be judged on the basis of the number of cases, as it emanates from the linkage to VERs.

An exporter informed that he is suspected of dumping generally faces an easy choice. Either problems are avoided through raised prices, which provide a higher profit margin but reduce sales, or there will be a costly legal process, the outcome of which is more or less predetermined. Subsequent to the verdict, the firm must count on a duty and cannot expect a higher profit per unit on its remaining sales. The social costs have already been commented on in Chapter 4.

As the competitive pressure builds up in the Single Market, there may gradually be greater demand for protectionism against outsiders. Domestic firms squeezed by competition from other EC countries cannot seek protection against them, but the door remains open for support against outsiders. The abolition of subsidies in defence of competitors within the EC may make funds available over the budget. While external competition hurts producers, consumers are normally the primary beneficiaries. As usual, the latter are poorly organized, and seldom have much to say. If a monetary union is implemented, the loss of mechanisms to adjust exchange rates may make external barriers the most convenient tool to cushion the impact of shocks that hit the member countries asymmetrically.

With declining applicability for the most-favoured-nation principle, trading partners are not all treated in the same way. In fact, the risk of raised barriers in the EC varies considerably between regions. The EFTA countries ought to be safe although, in practice, firms from these countries may still be discriminated against in public procurement. The Mediterranean countries outside the EC, as well as Eastern Europe, should also be in a relatively favourable position. This is due both to historical links and to the importance for the EC itself of stimulating improved economic performance in these regions. The developing countries covered by the Lomé convention will similarly retain their preferential access to the EC. The effects on most other developing countries will hinge crucially on the direction of the Community's policies with respect to textiles and agriculture.

The remaining actors are those in North America and East Asia. The inclusion of Mexico in NAFTA has probably been speeded up by the desire to strengthen the US bargaining position *vis-à-vis* a unified Europe. As in Europe, North American integration is accompanied by demands for external barriers. Considerable pressure can be exerted between these players on a bilateral basis, however, which should eventually result in cooperation rather than confrontation. East Asia is in a weaker position. There are several factors which make East Asian countries prone to discrimination in the EC. The following factors might speak for intensified discrimination in the EC of imports from East Asia.

- Bilateral trade is imbalanced in favour of East Asia, and is relatively less important for the EC than for Asia – as it amounts to a smaller share of total trade for the former (Anderson 1991).
- The limited exchange on all levels between Europe and East Asia, compared with that between the United States and East Asia, accounts for limited countervailing forces to protectionist sentiments in Europe (van Agt 1993).
- The greater competition expected in the EC for products based on high intensity in capital, technology and human skills will build up pressure for barriers against competitive outsiders. With resistance against barriers directed at the United States, and the EFTA countries integrated with the EC, such forces will target Japan and the ANIEs.
- The demand for protectionism is likely to be particularly evident in consumer electronics and related fields of industrial electronics. Rapid technological progress makes such products increasingly important, while European firms have great problems coping with the competition from more efficient East Asian producers.
- Irrespective of 1992, the need of the United States to achieve balance in its external trade forces East Asian countries, with their concentration on the US market, to diversify their exports away from it. As long as the currencies of the ANIEs remain pegged to the dollar, European markets then become relatively more lucrative. As import quotas in the EC are filled, Asian exports will appear more threatening and the demand for protectionist measures against them increases.
- The French government, which has advocated higher external protection as the barriers between the member countries are dissolved, gained support for that position with the EC membership of Greece, Spain and Portugal. Countries with less advanced industries are generally the most averse towards competition. The south European countries also have a lot to gain from reducing imports from Asia in, for example, leather, footwear, textiles, clothing and steel. A strong desire to support development in East European countries may provide arguments for closing out Asian competition. Figure 5.4 showed that the EC's imports from developing countries shifted the most towards Asia in the 1980s, with Europe in second place.
- Protectionist instruments are already available which can be effectively used for selective discrimination of imports. This puts protectionists in the favourable position of merely intensifying

the existing framework, while the burden of overturning it lies with those in favour of liberalization.

The risk of European isolationism will probably be much influenced by the degree to which the 1992 programme turns out to be beneficial for the EC itself. Given that the envisaged mobility in investment and labour diminishes the pockets of idle resources within the Community, the support for insularity will decline. It may also be noted that Germany, the main industrial power in the EC, at present focuses on its domestic crisis and internal liberalization of the EC in order, for example, to obtain suitable product standards. The country is a firm opponent of protectionism, and once such tasks have been overcome it should devote more attention to external relations. Nevertheless, one may expect the many different perceptions within the Community to account for a continuous struggle concerning external policy. The extent to which GATT is allowed to play an effective role, which in itself depends a great deal on the EC, is likely to influence the outcome crucially.

Even in the event that protectionists do prevail over free traders, it must be asked whether barriers represent a 'viable' strategy to keep East Asian producers out of the Single Market. For a number of reasons, the probable answer is 'no'. It is only possible to fend a certain percentage of a reduced sales volume, while export markets cannot be protected. In a more complex system, the sheltering of one producer will hurt another downstream. Control on steel imports damages automobile factories, tariffs on chips raise costs for computer manufacturers, etc. The costs of protectionism will ultimately not only be spread thinly among unsuspecting consumers, but will be felt intensively by producers as well. Finally, we have the role of direct investment.

5.7 JAPANESE DIRECT INVESTMENT IN EUROPE

As already noted, there was a great spurt of Japanese direct investment in the EC in the late 1980s. Many others have also entered the Community, and the Japanese are not the largest investors. The Americans have achieved a greater presence, and European firms operate across the various national economies as well.[8] This section nevertheless singles out the role of the Japanese. Their investment deserves special attention because of both the imbalanced interactions between Europe and Japan and the special features of Japanese direct investment in terms of technology and

130

organization. The Japanese are being followed by some other Asians into Europe, notably the Koreans, but their investments are so far much less significant.

Before investigating the pattern and characteristics of Japanese direct investment in Europe, let us briefly consider certain features of the European economies. Germany is undoubtedly the industrial core with a strong and modern manufacturing sector. Of the other countries in the Community, The Netherlands is strategically located and has a highly advanced chemical industry which relies on a successful emphasis on R&D as well as a range of innovations. France has traditionally been strong in heavy engineering, weaponry, aircraft and vehicles, but its industry encounters difficulties in the application of modern technology. Italy is in a similar situation, while the decline of domestic industry has progressed even further in Great Britain. Several studies have demonstrated the crisis of the innovating capability, especially in the UK, resulting in a worsening record for industries such as motor vehicles and machinery (Dunning 1990; Law 1991).

The role of the public sector, and its relations with industry, varies a great deal between the European economies. It is fair to speak of a consensus concerning the prevalence of a 'legal culture' in Germany which facilitates communication between the public sector and industry (Hancher and Reute 1987; Osterman 1988). There are particularly favourable, informal networks between corporations, research institutes and public institutions which upgrade the technology. Chemicals, aerospace, mechanical and electrical engineering industries have been targets of ambitious public programmes in this respect (Streit 1987). France also has well-developed informal links, which appear to serve partly as a leverage for state intervention and influence and partly as a basis for information-sharing (Cawson et al. 1987). In Great Britain, interactions between policy makers and industry have proliferated industrial demands for privileges (Appleby and Bessant 1987).

The source of competitiveness varies as well. Southern Europe has relatively low wages and relies on labour-intensive production. Northern Europe has sophisticated industry and service sectors, and large stocks of capital and skilled labour. However, Table 3.1 indicates a lower level of general education in comparison with Japan. All European countries lag behind both the United States and Japan in the share of the working force with university degrees. Of the countries included in the table, only Sweden and Germany have a relatively large share of graduates in engineering, while France, the UK and Belgium tend to focus on law and commerce. In the case of crime rates, Table 4.1 similarly demonstrated a much weaker record than that of Japan, although Europe does not perform as badly as the United States. In the labour markets, northern Europe typically has strong and demanding labour unions. As in the United States, work and remuneration are based on individual rather than group efforts. Such comparisons represent sweeping generalizations, however. Historical and cultural factors account for heterogeneous conditions even within Europe.

Most Japanese investments in Europe have gone into services such as finance and insurance. We have already noted some of the special motives for Japanese direct investment in Europe in the financial field – the Euro-dollar markets, the restrictions at home, the need to service industrial partners, etc. The Japanese have scaled down financial activities in Europe in recent years, however. This is partly due to the financially troublesome situation in Japan, and the pressure to fulfil the requirements of the Bank of International Settlements, and partly to the difficulties which confront them in Europe. The major future motivation for Japanese banks to be present in Europe appears to be related to their functions as nodes in corporate information networks.

As the importance of services expands in the production of virtually any good, the dividing line between sectors is becoming less applicable. However, manufacturing remains the crucial activity in determining the economic strength and welfare of nations. Except for finance, manufacturing is the main destination for Japanese direct investment in Europe. The sector accounts for some 15–30 per cent in the flow to each of the host countries in Table 5.10, except for Luxembourg. Thus, the following discussion focuses on manufacturing, while the connection to services should be kept in mind.

Several studies have analysed the motives of Japanese operations in Europe, and tried to rank them.[9] Most commonly emphasized are the globalization of business operations, changing conditions in Japan itself as well as in the United States, and the opportunities or risks associated with the European integration process. Through direct investment, Japanese firms hope to qualify as insiders and price and sell more freely within the Single Market. Smaller attractions are reported in local technology, which contrasts with the motives for entering the United States. Europe is more commonly referred to as a source of knowledge in the field of design

Table 5.10 Geographical and sectoral distribution of Japanese direct investment in Europe, 1951–89 (cumulative) (per cent)

	UK	France	Germany	The Netherlands	Luxembourg
Food	0.6	4.6	0.2	0.4	0.0
Chemicals	0.6	1.3	10.9	2.7	0.0
Machinery	3.2	8.0	4.0	2.5	0.3
Electrical machinery	4.9	4.1	9.9	4.8	0.0
Transport machinery	2.9	1.8	0.7	1.5	0.0
Manufacturing total	14.4	29.3	28.9	15.0	0.4
Commerce	7.8	21.1	39.6	12.0	0.0
Bank and Insurance	52.3	10.0	13.2	50.4	96.3
Service	2.7	10.2	2.3	9.9	0.3
Real estate	10.7	16.8	0.6	11.9	0.4
Total (billion US$)	15.8	2.9	3.4	10.1	5.4
Share[a]	35.1	6.4	7.7	22.4	12.0

Source: Ministry of Finance 1990
Note: [a] In percentage of all Japanese direct investment in Europe.

and marketing. Generalizations tend to argue that the Japanese establish projects which are completely foreign owned and focus on activities in which they have a marked technological advantage *vis-à-vis* European firms. There are many accusations of 'screwdriver' operations, which provide little value added but assemble parts and components imported from suppliers at home or in third countries.[10]

The undertaking of direct investment is also related to public responses. The stages passed through by Japanese electronics firms in Europe, for example, display a clearcut interplay with policy actions. In electronics in particular, the establishment of assembly plants followed upon complaints to the Commission about the expansion of inexpensive Japanese exports provided in large volumes. The success of the assembly plants was countered by the imposition of local content rules, which enforced a greater integration with local industry. Japanese suppliers then followed their core firms to the Community, making the question of what actually is local content difficult to answer. This has contributed to the 'herd behaviour' of the Japanese, with a clustering of activities in certain locations.

The relationship between barriers to trade and the undertaking of direct investment is far from straightforward. Focusing on the possibility of lobbying, Bhagwati (1988) suggests that multinational firms counteract protectionism because they are damaged by barriers to trade as both buyers and sellers. However, there is no empirical evidence of a major impact in this respect. Alternatively, direct investment may bring unwanted competition for local industry that is possibly stronger than that represented by exports. Unless it is possible to neutralize the efficiency of direct investment, this will then discourage demands for too large trade barriers. Under such circumstances, the prospects of receiving direct investment would consequently impose a discipline on trade policies.[11] On the other hand, the selective nature of the new protectionism enables discrimination against foreign investors, not only against exporters, for example through the threat of antidumping proceedings.

To the extent that direct investment provides advantages for a host country, there may be a complementary relationship between the adoption of trade barriers and the undertaking of direct investment. Once again, direct investment may offer employment opportunities, corporate tax revenue, technological spillover effects to local industry, etc. The literature on content protection explores how trade policy can be used to influence the imports of parts and components (Grossman 1981; Hollander 1987). By introducing various forms of performance requirements, particularly local content rules, host countries may raise the gains of domestic industry from direct investment.[12] In certain cases, the objective may be partly to reduce the efficiency of foreign investors.

The interplay between European host countries and Japanese investors has additional dimensions. There are several alternative countries to invest in, which have varying characteristics and policy objectives. The continued integration process, particularly technical standardization and the scrapping of administrative barriers, increases the flexibility of firms' location decisions. Smaller impediments to trade across national boundaries diminish the importance of selling on the market of the host country itself. As of the late 1980s, the Japanese subsidiaries disposed of about half their output on host countries' markets and the rest in the other EC countries (Kume and Totsuka 1991). This figure is similar to that recorded for firms that originate in other countries.

Table 5.10 shows that Japanese direct investment is now fairly well distributed across Europe. This contrasts with the situation of the past, when projects were located mainly in Great Britain. There are obvious advantages associated with investment in this country, including the limited cultural and linguistic barrier, as it resembles the United States the most – a country with which the majority of Japanese firms entering Europe are acquainted. In addition, there is high political stability, many other attractive firms and activities are present, and generous public incentives are offered. Southern Europe has equally clearcut advantages in the form of low labour costs, on which Spain in particular capitalizes. Portugal, Greece and Ireland are unable to attract much investment because of their more peripheral locations, which mean less accessibility to the major markets in the Community.

The determinants of the pattern of direct investment across the main host countries in Europe are less obvious. Like the UK, The Netherlands and Germany have stable and mostly congenial regimes, while the attitudes of France are mixed and subject to change. These countries have received about the same amount of Japanese direct investment, and there are no clearcut differences in terms of traditional comparative advantages. However, the competitiveness of their domestic industries varies a great deal because of differences in experience, competence and industrial organization. How does this affect the pattern of investment and its interplay with the host economies?

Let us consider the characteristics and distribution of Japanese direct investment in manufacturing in Europe somewhat more closely. The focus is on Germany, the UK, The Netherlands and France, which are the most important European host countries in this sector. In addition, let us distinguish between the four major industries: machinery, transport, electronics and chemicals. These are all much influenced by the acess to rapidly changing technology. Firms must either shelter their knowledge and capitalize on it before it is diffused to competitors, or get access to that of others. Copying technology is more difficult in chemicals than in the other sectors, however, as it is embodied in production processes rather than products. Looking at revealed comparative advantage, i.e. net exports, Germany is the leading European producer in all four industries. In chemicals, The Netherlands is almost equally competitive. Japan, on the other hand, is strong in all industries except for chemicals.

The competitiveness and quality of local industry are known to influence the degree of foreign control in affiliates. The investors' characteristics are equally important. Consider the choice of entry mode by the Japanese firms in the different industries, shown in Table 5.11. Greenfield operations dominate almost exclusively in transport machinery and electrical machinery. In semiconductors, there is actually 100 per cent foreign ownership in all Japanese factories in Europe. The pattern is somewhat mixed in machinery, while in chemicals greenfield operations account for only 30 per cent and joint ventures make up 50 per cent of the total. The shares of acquisitions and participations are much larger in this industry as well. Thomsen and Nicolaides (1991) and Narula and Gugler (1991) concluded that access to European technology and expertise has been a prime motivation for Japanese direct investment in chemicals within Europe.

Table 5.11 Japanese entry modes in Europe, major industries (per cent)

Industry	Greenfield	Joint ventures	Acquisitions	Participations
Chemicals	30	50	10	10
Machinery	58	32	4	7
Electrical machinery	70	18	9	4
Transport machinery	80	10	0	10

Source: Thomsen and Nicolaides 1991

The locational pattern of Japanese direct investment in these four industries is indicated in Table 5.12 for 1985–9. A reverse relationship emerges between home and host country competitiveness, the latter estimated on the basis of net exports (Andersson 1992c). In machinery, the UK, The Netherlands and France, which have relatively weak revealed comparative advantages, obtain the bulk of Japanese direct investment. The major destination in transport machinery is the UK, which is the least competitive country in that industry. In electrical machinery where all the other European countries are weak relative to Germany, the UK and The Netherlands receive the largest investments, while Germany is well behind in third place. The chemical industry, however, is instead characterized by direct investment in the strongest European countries, i.e. Germany and The Netherlands.

These observations illustrate the crucial role of the race for technology, knowledge and competitiveness in the undertaking, nature and location of direct investment – in this case Japanese direct investment in Europe.[13] To the extent that technology and learning

Table 5.12 Japanese direct investment in Europe, major countries and industries, 1985–9 (cumulative) (million US$)

Industry	UK	France	Germany	The Netherlands	Spain
Food	91	103	7	39	0
Chemicals	101	25	356	211	83
Machinery	449	211	74	231	29
Electrical machinery	652	75	244	482	60
Transport machinery	445	50	15	151	349
Total manufacturing	2,000	634	772	1,361	598

Source: Ministry of Finance 1990

effects spill over to actors in the host country, Japanese investments should strengthen European countries in activities where they are relatively weak, not where they are strong. At the same time, the Japanese appear to limit the diffusion to domestic actors carefully, and the more so the more competitive they are. By operating within relatively uncompetitive countries, the Japanese should speed up the convergence of the European economies. At the same time, their clustering behaviour will lead to new patterns of polarization. On the whole, however, the Japanese may not directly advance the European technological frontier. To the extent that direct investment does spur such advancement, it occurs through an indirect effect, because industries in the most competitive European countries would shape up when their 'Japanese' competitors in other European countries do.

Where they are relatively weak, however, the Japanese do merge and cooperate with strong Europeans. In many cases, the Japanese are likely to benefit the most from such interaction, because they are effective in the commercial application of technology. This is associated with their overlapping information systems, mentioned above. In the specific case of joint ventures with Europeans, Mayes (1990) notes worries about technology transfers to Japan.

Concerning the attitudes and actions of policy makers, with respect to direct investment, the interests of member countries in the Community are contradictory by nature. For the host country, great gains may be extracted from direct investment. This is even more true to the extent that imports to the Community are impeded, as the foreign investors provide an output whose supply is restricted. Those countries which do not act as hosts, on the other hand, may see the efficiency and competitiveness of their own industries undermined by direct investment in their neighbour country, and end up importing from the country in the Community instead of Japan. Under such circumstances, there are strong incentives for competition to attract foreign investments.[14]

Such public competition typically favours an optimal allocation of investment internationally. As shown in Andersson (1991a), the country in which a certain project generates the largest net benefit is the one which obtains it. The level of that country's gains is determined by the quality of its opportunities relative to those of the second best country, and by the mobility of investment, while the composition of gains depends on the country's priorities with respect to, for example, foreign exchange earnings, tax revenue and externalities. As declining barriers within the Community make the member countries increasingly close substitutes as locations, one may expect them to capture a diminishing share of the rents that emanate from barriers to trade.

Lehmann (1992) discusses responses of the EC countries to the challenge of Japanese direct investment. Some collaborate, some compete and some confront the Japanese. Disputes over the location of their car manufacturing in the UK entered into Brussels several years ago. The Danes, the Irish or the Dutch are not eager to pay more for Japanese cars in order to permit the French and the Italians to avoid adjustments. Because the member countries are historically and culturally sovereign, and have different structures, the variation in attitudes will not easily go away.

The more effective the external barriers of the EC become, the more desirable direct investment will be, and the fiercer the competition between individual EC countries. Of course, it can be expected that the EC will try to coordinate polices with regard to inward investment. However, protectionism coupled with demands for stringency against foreign investors creates strong incentives for the individual member countries to cheat on the group. Similarly, it becomes desirable for local firms to let the outsiders in through profitable partnerships. Thus, direct investment should continue to flow into the EC and escape with rents created by protectionism. If the EC, on the other hand, was to succeed in both shutting out imports and deterring inward investment, the desired goods would become even more scarce and expensive. This would produce the worst possible result for the EC, as consumers and buyers of intermediate goods would have to get used to the second or third best.

138

5.8 ADDITIONAL COSTS

Except for the situation in the EC itself, there is an additional set of factors which will make discriminatory trade and investment policies costly for Europeans. These concern the future importance of East Asian markets. The doubts about the openness of the EC, together with the prospects of a less accessible US market, already spur a growing emphasis by the Asians on their own region. As discussed in Chapter 4, this is not merely a defensive reaction. In spite of Japan's present economic dominance, the region is populated by a number of peoples who are not going to rest, and who will not allow the Japanese to become too self-complacent. The Koreans are already well on their way, and the overseas Chinese in East Asia know better than the Japanese how to exploit the opportunities in China.

A closed Community allows European firms to continue their neglect of East Asia or, at least, not to try sufficiently to adapt there. The importance of a long-term commitment to the Japanese market has already been pointed out. A powerful language barrier, alien business and cultural practices, the multi-layer distribution system, high costs of housing and living – particularly for expatriates – and so on often mean a long period of years before economic rewards materialize. East Asians are careful with product quality and enjoy stable and reliable business relationships. In order to share in the future growth of the region, it is time for Europeans to be active there today.

There are additional reasons why not moving ahead into East Asia can become very costly. Success in East Asia today may be necessary for survival tomorrow. The Japanese compete fiercely within their home market before going abroad, and then race against each other in international crusades. Those foreign firms which have managed to withstand competition abroad are often precisely those which have weathered it in Japan already. Not least because of the vigorous competition among domestic and foreign firms which try to enter Japan, there is an intense technological upgrading and learning going on in this market. Staying away means that Western firms forgo a crucial stimulus for their organizations as a whole. Without experience within East Asia, Westerners will continue to learn only in their own sphere, while East Asians learn throughout the whole playing field.

Not only is a solid position at home the basis for Japanese

corporations abroad. If the growing East Asian region is left to sharpen the commercial weaponry of Japanese and other East Asian firms exclusively, they will be in an immensely stronger position to start out from the day that attacks are launched on the Single Market anyway. Without establishments in East Asia, Westerners will find it increasingly difficult to compete head on in Europe and elsewhere.

On this basis, the opportunities that arise from the creation of the Single Market should outweigh the fears of a 'fortification' of Europe through taxes or NTBs. In other words, the risks should subside with the realization that 'armaments' would be costly not only for outsiders but more so for Europe itself. If nations and international bodies are sufficiently motivated by a concern for social welfare, the EC should be an open market place. If not, there will be a worsening of the economic and political troubles in Europe, which will interfere with its abilities to handle its interior issues as well. In the early 1990s, the interest of the Japanese in Europe has, again, been cooling. They will continue to be present, to learn and to extract gains. But in terms of real emphasis for the future, one may wonder whether Asians will eventually feel better off in an expanding home region rather than in a troubled and inward-looking West.

6

POLICY IMPLICATIONS

The developments discussed in this book raise various policy issues.
With few exceptions, the planned economies are gone, if not yet
buried. It may be expected that those who rely purely on spon-
taneous market responses will soon belong to an equally outdated
generation. This follows not only from the example of East Asia.
Many values are not taken into account by private actors, and
positive as well as negative 'external' effects pass unnoticed in the
absence of some form of coordination. It is well known that
knowledge partly takes the form of a public good. Moreover, the
ambitions of different individuals will be more or less hampered if
they counteract each other. Such considerations are becoming
increasingly important as the pace of technological progress quickens
and the life-span of new products becomes shorter within the
expanding networks of economic interactions.

This chapter argues that the issues of our time require parallel
efforts to secure an open world economy and to stimulate greater
human skills – particularly the ability to engineer solutions to
common problems. The first section is concerned with the international agenda, after which the focus is on the need for a European
agenda for East Asia. The path chosen by Western Europe in this
respect is of crucial importance for several reasons. These include
the changing role of the United States, the connections to Europe's
internal restructuring and the fact that Europe has a missing link
with East Asia. These factors set the stage for a delicate interplay
between the European position and the future direction of the
world trade system as a whole.

6.1 THE INTERNATIONAL AGENDA

The 'new' world economy is characterized by an increased capacity to utilize resources effectively and improved prospects for social well-being. At the same time, there are frustrated means of exchange and a lack of guidance on how to proceed. This section presents the following interrelated components of an international agenda to deal with the situation: acceptance of East Asia; learning on the part of the West; seizure of opportunities in East Asia; establishment of an open means of exchange; policy coordination; and finally the need to resume responsibility.

Acceptance of East Asia

There is a deep-rooted animosity between Western countries and the Far East, especially Japan. Wilkinson (1989) reviews how this has evolved over time. Misconceptions and criticisms have flourished on both sides. After Japan was 'opened up' in the 1860s, and again after the Second World War, however, the Japanese have conscientiously tried to study and learn from the West. This has in no way been reciprocated.

Even today, the progress in Japan and other East Asian countries is frequently claimed to represent a temporary and brittle phenomenon. It is true that Japan experiences acute economic difficulties, and question marks surround long-term preferences. There will soon be a greater proportion of elderly people and the young may decide to spend more and enjoy longer holidays rather than work long hours. The financial liberalization and the growing presence of foreigners in Japan also account for change. Firms are reported to have less stable relations among each other and with main banks,[1] more employees choose to work for foreign companies, retailer–customer relations are loosening up even in the countryside, etc.

Despite such well-publicized considerations, we had nevertheless better become accustomed to the strong economic performance of the Pacific Basin. The fact that the value of Tokyo's stock exchange was more than halved between 1989 and 1992, for example, is part of a global process of contraction and normalization which follows on the bursting of the financial bubbles built up during the 1980s. In the same way as Japan absorbed and recovered from the first oil price shock with an astonishing speed, it is once again managing the financial crisis relatively well. The public sector refrains from running up a major deficit, consumers are adjusting to what is perceived as a permanently lower level of consumption, corporate management reduces dividends and cuts the remuneration and benefits of senior executives while, at the same time, collective attempts of adaptation are spread throughout organizations.

Japan's competitiveness in production, trade and investment will not be more than temporarily impeded by the current problems. It will take time before preferences with respect to work, family and savings change. The balance between Japanese expansion at home and abroad, on the other hand, will be determined by a range of yet unsettled factors. These include the pace with which a rising yen makes exports from home more expensive, the options that arise in the international competition for R&D and its application, as well as the rules which govern the trade system as a whole.

Other countries in the Pacific Basin have a long way to go before being able to reach a satisfactory economic situation. The less developed countries provide profitable investment and sales opportunities, but will also offer fresh rivalry, especially in the decades ahead. The population of the Pacific Basin presents an enormous growth potential, particularly in China, but also in countries such as Indonesia and Vietnam. In spite of many differences, the competition from their neighbours is viewed by the Japanese as a follow-up to their own methods, and therefore is understandable. At the same time, if nothing else does, it will haunt and inspire the Japanese.

Learning on the part of the West

Accepting the development in East Asia, the Western economies must actively engage themselves in it. Any meaningful action must be based on knowledge and an understanding of the basis of its success, however. There is little doubt that the managing of human skills plays a key role. In particular, the East Asian record draws attention to the economic importance of human relations for learning, creativity and reliability.

The Japanese appear particularly skilful at being able to channel information and synchronize efforts between, for example, workers and employees, retailers and consumers, or separate firms and departments. This contributes to, among other things, high quality and the rapid transformation of modern technologies into demanded products. Although it takes time to establish consensus about overriding decisions, flexibility and adaptability in response to

143

changing conditions have in themselves become key features of Japanese organizations.

The East Asian record is not an artifact of government planning. Rather, the role of government is symptomatic of society as a whole. Dealing with this challenge from a Western perspective is similarly not primarily a question of public action. Nevertheless, governments take a special responsibility. Above all, the traditional public task of securing macroeconomic balance remains of high priority. Weak budgets, emerging as a result of the inability of governments to handle their own affairs, continue to be a major cause of current account deficits. Price instability and high interest rates damage long-term projects and undermine the prospects for lasting relationships.

Apart from managing the macroeconomy, however, governments cannot neglect the nature of micro level processes. This is not a question of detailed planning. Nor does it motivate transfer payments or subsidies which worsen public finances. The government's principal microeconomic duty is to monitor and protect the character of incentives. The question is whether the costs and benefits that confront individuals approximate those which are inflicted on society as a whole. In this respect, the West does have traditions. Stretching back to Aristotle, there is a model of an 'organic state' whose primary obligation is that of morals. Thomas Jefferson, for example, feared that influential interest groups would take over through government, and advocated a state which supports and defends a fabric of local units which are best informed of the needs of society.[2] During the nineteenth century, such ideas were transformed and rearranged to fit the liberal defence of individual freedom from public authority, as well as from the traditional restraints of society in a more general sense.

The growing importance of modern technology, and the increasing risks, costs and economies of scale and scope which are involved in its development, raise new demands for strategic alliances and joint efforts. At the same time, it becomes less productive to standardize job assignments. Discretion and the ability to improvise the synchronization of different skills appear as an advantage throughout the production process. Inconsistencies and mistrust between individuals, organizations, departments or ethnic groups impede and undermine the competitiveness of societies.

Although one can observe its virtues or the conditions under which it seems to be fostered, and sense the pleasure of the security that it brings, trust remains a volatile concept. It is often contrasted with the prevalence of opportunism, which requires investment to deal with moral hazard or adverse selection problems. Trust implies a small perceived risk that a counterpart may cheat, even when times get tough and/or temptations appear on the scene. It has been argued in this book that there may be different equilibria in human inter-actions. The more that trustworthiness represents a universally acknowledged and appreciated trait in society, the greater the damage caused to future business opportunities from the violation of trust in the first place. In this sense, trust is a 'common good' which makes it relatively easy to establish reliability between economic counterparts.

The West is certainly not East Asia, and should not try to be that either. However, there are lessons to be learned which apply in varying degree. European countries are different from the United States, as well as being different from each other. Germany, for example, has a good deal of the committed links and intense exchange of information which are found in Japan, while Great Britain resembles the United States. In all societies, however, incentives are subject to change, and the economic and social environment is under all circumstances influenced by policies. Moving in a desirable direction may in many ways hinge on public action, as private interests cannot resume full responsibility for stimuli that benefit all the actors in an economy.

Western countries need to pay attention to the incentives for human capital formation in general, and the reinforcement of reliable relationships in particular. Policy makers should scrutinize the behaviour that is promoted by the educational and judicial systems, and transmitted through the customs and guidelines adopted within factor markets. There can be little doubt that modern technologies will punish those social contexts which rely on individual 'realms' of expertise and prestige, and favour those which stimulate joint action. In Western labour markets, for example, highly specialized employees tend to be promoted and remunerated on the basis of individual performance rather than the success of projects as a whole. Arrow (1974) noted that this may account for short-term efficiency gains but inflicts long-term losses due to the obstruction of information.

Altering the premises for human interaction may seem an abstract and impossible task. However, the challenge is simply to free those energies which are restricted when the members of a team fail to engineer common strategies.

The seizure of opportunities in East Asia

It will not be sufficient for Western economies simply to restructure themselves. East Asians are constantly learning both in the East and in the West. The collection of information cannot be only one way. Western firms must take on East Asian markets not only to adjust in order to be successful there, but also to improve their operations as a whole.

In addition, Western governments must probably continue to exert pressure on East Asian countries to 'open up'. This may be a constructive exercise for several reasons. Japan, and certainly South Korea and Taiwan among the ANIEs, continue to operate a number of NTBs as well as DTBs which result from government policies as well as corporate practices. These establish discrimination against foreigners, either because that is the conscious goal or indirectly because foreigners are not organized in a way which allows them to deal with such requirements effectively.

Unlike tariffs and NTBs, however, DTBs do not systematically switch domestic expenditure away from imports, but instead hamper the efficiency of the economy. The elimination of structural impediments such as the Japanese multi-layer distribution system will free capital and labour to enter, for example, the home electronics and computer industries. Thus, the liberalizing economy will become more competitive, unless, of course, new regulations or distortions are introduced. There will be greater access to goods, services and investment in general, including those provided from abroad. The effect will be better prospects for trade in both directions, which is what we should expect.

This is no reason not to press for the break up of structural impediments, as access to the Japanese market would be better for everybody – foreigners as well as the Japanese. A scheme for entering Japan however, must not push for discriminatory measures which favour some foreigners at the expense of others. It is similarly detrimental to request the undertaking of specific transactions which violate the virtues of Japanese society rather than exploiting them. Finally, pressure on Japan must not be an excuse for protection of one's own market. The machinery for influencing the policies of another country must be explicitly designed not to serve as a temptation for implementing trade barriers at home.

Western success in Japan can never be achieved through government action alone. For Western firms to make the necessary efforts, and to account for an acceptable public support, the West itself must acknowledge that it has no option than to stay open itself – or see its economic greatness creep into the pages of the history books.

Establish open means of exchange

The argument put forward in favour of protection is normally that it will only provide assistance in the short run. Normally, however, those awarded the privilege of subsidy – management as well as labour – in order to acquire time to adjust, begin to think that adjustment may not be necessary at all. Firms forming cartels with competitors in order to gather the political clout to shut others out spend their energies on defending privileges rather than achieving competitiveness. When competition finally comes, those led to believe that they can avoid it will be particularly badly prepared.

The new protectionism attempted by the West is not going to work. Beyond the ordinary gains from trade there are super-gains associated with the feedback of information and discipline on the incentives that confront private actors as well as governments. These gains cannot be compromised. The organizational structures of the Japanese and other East Asians were borne out of a tenacious effort to become competitive. It is through trade and investment that the West is exposed to the power of their improvements, and are induced to learn.

An open trade policy must be combined with macroeconomic policies which support economic stability and competitive cost levels. If, as in the United States for the last decade, total output is lower than the absorption of resources through investment and consumption, the difference must come from the rest of the world, and be reflected in a current account deficit. This is unavoidable as long as the savings deficit prevails. Unless there are exogenous shocks in the terms of trade or consumer preferences, such imbalances can only be corrected through appropriate macroeconomic policy adjustments in the country running the deficit, or surplus. Rather than serving as a cure, protection aggravates the problems by mitigating the pressure for improved productivity and slowing growth. To borrow a comment from George Stigler: 'the bad thing about depressions is not that people starve, but that they think badly'. The same is true for trade deficits.

The process of regional liberalization, in North America and in

Europe, will help to dismantle barriers which lock resources into inefficient activities. However, renewed and continuous efforts will be required to make this development compatible with support of the trading system as a whole. At least, the long conflict over the Uruguay Round may have brought the realization that the open world trade system cannot be taken for granted but must be fought for. It is not enough with symbolic improvements. A real strengthening of the links between emerging 'regional groups', in North America, Western Europe, Asia and the third world, takes substantial reform.

It is sometimes argued that East Asia, which enjoys the largest trade surpluses and is the most targeted by new protectionism, needs such reform the most. Both Japan and the ANIEs have undertaken a certain amount of liberalization, but there appears to be a lack of affirmative moves, not least by the Japanese. This applies to the need to achieve accessibility and transparency at home as well as taking initiatives in multilateral negotiations. The passive stance is partly associated with the weaknesses of a group-oriented system. Organizations improve bit by bit, but breaking up entire structures is another thing. That often takes individual leadership.

In the absence of a more open Japanese economy and a strengthened multilateral trade system, however, the Japanese and other East Asians will continue to go to the West to learn. Imai (1993) predicts that Japanese firms will eventually internationalize not only production but R&D activities as well, in order to be truly efficient on a global scale. It will be Westerners who refrain from learning in the East and who seek to mitigate the impetus of change. Rather than stimulating search processes and the mobilization of energies in public and private organizations for productive purposes, Westerners will end up wasting their talent on calls for protective measures.

Policy coordination

The combination of market imperfections and destructive policy interference in goods and factor markets, coupled with inconsistent fiscal and monetary policies in different countries, continues to account for a major misallocation of resources. The global patterns of savings and investments are badly mismatched, and fail to foster welfare for the world as a whole. Apart from the need to establish appropriate and reliable rules for free trade, there is a great need for improved coordination of macroeconomic policies. This has shown up, for example, in the processes of regional integration and regular meetings between the leaders of the major industrialized countries (the Group of Seven).

The gains of coordination are even greater where there is no functioning trade at all. The Rio Summit in 1992 achieved an awareness of the connections between development and sustainable resource use, but also of the disparities that prevail in perceptions and consequently of the need for improved information. Environmental concerns are gradually becoming commercially relevant, but in the short term private firms as well as policy makers have strong incentives to hide averse effects, in order not to be forced to cope with them. The mobility of factors of production, as well as the cross-border nature of much pollution, makes it impossible to deal with the environment on a unilateral basis. Establishing sound management will require some form of compensation for environmental effects and resolution of conflicts between environmental agreements and the multilateral trade system. Unfortunately, impatience with the lack of action, together with the defensive reactions against East Asian dynamism, may instead result in barriers to commercial trade.

International policy coordination will also be required to help the formerly planned economies onto a path of revitalization and growth. The same applies to the mounting problems of poverty and stagnation in developing countries – inhabited by the vast majority of the world's overly young and rapidly growing population. In either case, the needs are too large for fragmented relief actions to make a difference. What is needed, rather than the provision of cash *per se*, is a coordination of domestic efforts and international actions which facilitate the provision of appropriate technologies and open up new opportunities for investment and trade. In addition, there is a continued demand for the effective formulation of international alliances on those occasions when the destructive sides of humanity take control. This is not only the case when the media expose the contrast between evil tyrants and starving children on the one hand and noble salvation troops on the other.

Great civilizations tend to forget about the danger of inner disarray, turmoil and destruction. History displays a sequence of social catastrophes, and there are poor and dark corners in the world. However, even in the wealthiest of societies, the human virtues of trust and reliability are steadily threatened. The weakest and most defenceless – often women, children and the disabled –

pay the price for human greed and lawlessness every day. Indeed, Western societies are currently demonstrating frightening tendencies in this respect. The enlightenment that characterized the aftermath of the Second World War is coming to an end as people begin to forget. A menacing tendency towards isolationism and intolerance is making itself felt in Europe, not least in Germany.

Japan has always had its violent and corrupt aspects as well, not least in the peculiar phenomenon of the *Yakusa*. Meanwhile, the legacy of 'underground' activities has expanded in the formerly planned economies, particularly the Russian Republic, and there is now an avalanche of organized crime. Hence, there is a legacy of brutality on many sides, and the illegal trade in drugs and weapons continues to rank among the largest fields of economic activity in the world. Paradoxically, it is conceivable that the ending of the Cold War and the internationalization of trade and investment might be accompanied by an unholy alliance of borderless vice and estrangement between peoples that are brought into contact with each other but who do not share any means of communication.

The need to resume responsibility

Although it may appear difficult to compare, developments in East Asia open up greater opportunities than risks. When trying to compete, the West must not run down those opportunities. Skills in the form of ability to utilize R&D more effectively, to share information and to be creative in how to satisfy consumer demands represent great assets which are much needed around the world.

No actor carries the sole responsibility for the world economy. On the contrary, realizing the potential of the 'new' world economy will require an improved capacity to share responsibilities. Without open means of exchange, future incomes will be reduced as the revitalizing processes of learning and adjustment are held back. Given the weakened US position, and the link that is missing among the major economic actors, it is an immediate task for Europe to formulate an adequate agenda for East Asia.

6.2 DEMANDS ON A EUROPEAN AGENDA FOR EAST ASIA

Europe is confronted with a massive agenda. Most attention has so far been devoted to internal restructuring, in the form of the Single

Market and the EU, which is still subject to a number of difficulties. The intense exchange with the EFTA countries underlines the importance of either the creation of a functioning EEA or an expansion of the Community. The urgency of establishing stable and productive conditions in Eastern Europe similarly calls for a rapid implementation of non-discriminatory trade with these countries.

Some might say that these issues have to be tackled one at a time. They are interrelated, however, and must be dealt with within one context. In particular, the urgent matters within Europe should not obscure the importance of a better planned and more imaginative European policy *vis-à-vis* East Asia. This grows partly out of Europe's own position on the East Asian agenda. East Asians are well prepared to benefit from the European market, while most Europeans are so engaged in creating it – and using it – that they neglect the opportunities in East Asia. This will most probably account for continuously growing imbalances in trade, investment and, most important, learning.

The relationship between Europe and East Asia is to a consider-able extent a matter of attitudes. For example, Japanese firms tend to view the other East Asian markets as stable and reliable, while European firms often view them as uncertain. However, Europeans enjoy a certain goodwill in East Asia compared with the Japanese. The attitudes that prevail in Europe today give rise to far too many misapprehensions and easy excuses for not trying to export and invest in Japan in particular. As noted by Commissioner Andriessen: 'It is increasingly clear that the development of European exports to Japan depends as much on the interest of Community companies in the market as on the removal of trade barriers.'[3]

Japan-bashing has the opposite effect of preventing Westerners from looking for opportunities. While many Americans, more or less in panic, are calling for the exclusion of Japanese interests, some Euro-peans take the equally dangerous and unwise viewpoint that 'what goes up, must come down'. Underlying such a relaxed attitude, there is partly an inadequate knowledge of Japan and partly a belief that Europe will become notably stronger post-1992, and/or that others can be hindered from exploiting the Single Market. Again, outsiders will benefit from its completion as well, at least in the absence of increased external protectionism, and there is unlikely to be any consistent and effective policy to exclude them. There is, in any case, no such policy which is favourable for the Community itself.

Instead of focusing on the fundamental sources of growth and welfare, strains are often associated with the threatening actions of others. Servan-Schreiber (1967) warned about growing United States dominance in European industry. Today, the issue is not that of 'too large' a foreign presence in Europe, as maintained by some, but rather the presence of too little exchange in both directions with respect to East Asia. Actions are needed to strengthen the capacity to exploit opportunities in trade and investment. This includes measures at the micro level which allow human efforts to be compatible. Improved relations in general with East Asian countries must also be promoted in order to overcome friction without resorting to destructive policies. On an overriding level, Europe needs to support an economic world order which facilitates free trade and capital movements. An appropriate policy *vis-à-vis* East Asia may provide the key to Europe's ability not only to cope with its external relations in general but also to deal with its internal issues.

The agenda must be devised on multiple levels. Trade and investments between two regions disparate in institutional and cultural conditions as well as geographical distance do not occur as an isolated phenomenon. The success of commercial interactions hinges on satisfactory information, and the ability to handle it. Information must be available regarding business opportunities and efficient ways to approach them. Progress in this respect will require a general expansion of relationships. It will take action on the part of many different players to achieve palpable results.

6.3 ITEMS ON A EUROPEAN AGENDA FOR EAST ASIA

This final section outlines a number of elements which may be regarded as particularly important on a European agenda for East Asia.

Provision of information

It is essential to acquire much better knowledge of, and access to information on, the European–East Asian relationship. This includes data on the nature of the shift in gravity that has taken place from the Atlantic to the Pacific, the new markets in East Asia, and the characteristics and consequences of the new competition from East Asian firms. Extensive study of these matters should facilitate a constructive approach to East Asia among policy makers, business people and academics in Europe.

The present perceptions of the way Japan or other East Asian countries are 'different' are almost entirely based on comparisons with the United States. Typically, major US universities have high powered centres on Japanese and East Asian studies. The limited activities of European universities in this direction put Europe at a disadvantage in interactions with East Asia. Universities and schools in Europe should therefore develop their curricula in order to make it possible for the next generation of policy makers and business people to acquire a better understanding of East Asia in general.

However, various parts of society should cooperate in order to identify the needs and how they can be met. While policy makers bear a certain responsibility for promoting socially valuable information, actually dismantling the causes of friction must ultimately be taken care of by private corporations. Their support, or request for, research and educational programmes directed at the region may also help to encourage an output which is of practical relevance.

A more vivid dialogue and better fora for contacts

Apart from improved information, livelier contacts between the regions are necessary to stimulate European exports and investments in East Asia. Partly as a result of the legacy of the Second World War, the Cold War and the US need for stable allies in the Far East, the United States has cooperated with East Asia for a long time. Numerous fora for discussion have been created, for government officials, business executives, trainees and academics. As contacts have multiplied and deepened, there is a greater understanding of opportunities as well as risks. At present, the United States has much more friction with Japan and the ANIEs than Europe has, but it is still a fact that the United States has managed to develop more intensive trade and investment contacts with the region. The following fora are examples of United States–East Asian contacts:

- The Pacific Basin Economic Council (PBEC), formed in 1967, brings together executives for annual conferences. It aims to

153

'improve business environments, strengthen the business enterprise system, generate new business opportunities, create new
business relationships, and increase trade and investment within
the Pacific Basin area'.

- The Pacific Free Trade and Development Conference (PAFTAD),
  which first convened in 1968, is an organization for academic
  economists.
- Since the early 1980s, a series of annual Pacific Economic
  Cooperation Conferences (PECC) has assembled government
  officials in a private capacity, as well as representatives of the
  academic and business sectors, for policy-oriented discussions.
- In 1989, the initiative was taken to upgrade the political level of
  Pacific meetings in order to make it possible to set up a forum
  for ministerial meetings.

The EC does run a Centre for Industrial Cooperation in Tokyo
together with the Japanese. This improves the opportunities for EC
business people to acquaint themselves with Japan. An Executive
Training programme finances an eighteen-month period in Japan
for young executives, and a special exchange programme invites EC
trainees for one week every year. Cooperation has also been
established between the EC and Japan in science and technology,
for instance concerning nuclear safeguards and environmental policy
coordination.[4] In ASEAN, Joint Investment Committees stimulate
European business activities. Sporadic meetings and exchange
programmes have also been organized to discuss, for example,
industrial exchange and human resource development. A trade and
economic cooperation agreement was signed with China in 1985
but, as in the case of Korea, contacts have mainly consisted of high-
level meetings and consultations. On the whole, the existing fora
are too small in relation to the needs, and represent too little
interaction on multiple levels.

Corporate strategies

European firms should devise and implement corporate strategies
which more consistently exploit the opportunities in East Asia.
Although East Asian markets are already large and profitable for
many European firms, they continue to attract little interest at
headquarters. Public exchange programmes of the type discussed
above can help to increase corporate awareness of East Asia, but
the major steps must be taken care of by business itself.

To improve their record, Western firms should study the long-term business strategies of Japanese and other East Asian firms. These include the success stories of foreign exporters and investors – including American ones – in their markets. A proper knowledge in this respect will require direct experience of the relevant structures within East Asia, and the fostering of interactions with local representatives. Firms should implement incentive programmes which enable employees actively to engage in work with East Asia. Skills of direct relevance to the region should be cultivated.[5] Trainee systems could be formed, and business experience from East Asia could account for special merit value for young executives in their careers. Market studies and other enquiries which usually precede exports and direct investment should be directed towards a better ascertainment of the opportunities in East Asia.

Competition in Europe

The integration process, if properly managed, will strengthen the European economy and the competitiveness of European firms. There will be greater scale advantages and improved means to handle common European problems. However, higher growth is primarily expected from an upgraded level of competition. This presupposes that intensified competition is not prevented through tacit collusion. In practice, both governments and private industry favour mergers, cartel building and extensive collaboration. It may be argued that such restructuring is wanted in order to manage the challenges of modern technology.

Socially valuable information-sharing and successful innovation grow out of the ability to construct mutually satisfactory but delicate dividing lines between domains of trust and cooperation on the one hand and those of rivalry on the other. The source of progress lies in the combination of joining forces to create knowledge and competing fiercely to exploit it in innovating activities – which draw on the special capabilities of individual actors. This pertains to relationships on various levels, between firms, departments and employers irrespective of national barriers. A synchronization of skills increases the potential output, while competition ensures that it is realized. Europe must accomplish both.

155

An open trade policy

Its external relations will have a direct bearing on the ability of the Community to settle its internal agenda. Allowing the Single Market to develop into a 'fortress' would counteract the expected favourable impact of the 1992 programme. Merging and/or collaborating huge firms within protected borders would exploit consumers, provide excessively expensive intermediate goods and apply distorted technologies. Isolated from impulses for dynamic change and trapped in technological decline, European firms would see fewer opportunities for expansion in foreign markets, including those in East Asia, and have less pressure to go there. In addition, external barriers would hurt growth prospects in liberalizing countries. Continued recession and instability in Eastern Europe will inevitably be incompatable with a prosperous Western Europe.

There would also be sharpened competition between individual countries or communities within the EC to attract sheltered activities, which would in turn lead to an escalation of tensions. External protectionism sets up centrifugal forces, not least in the heterogeneous Community where objectives and priorities differ. This could tear the EC apart from the inside, at least before the integration process has reached a stage where national considerations, as we know them now, have disappeared.

The attempt to 'manage' trade through bilateral pressures executed with new instruments is rising. Although the US remains the chief player in this, the external policy of the EC influences the path of others. The question of whether the United States will continue on a trail of escalating protectionism, or rebound against it, will be largely influenced by the European position. Likewise, it will take a constructive Europe for East Asian countries to become more open. That region should favour an open world trade system – but may lack the initiative to take the lead towards establishing it.

To the extent that the United States presses for unilateral advantages, only Europe can forcefully call for general openness. It has been suggested that public support is needed to identify 'obstacles which target foreigners specifically' in Japan. Consider the reception of foreign technology. R&D hinges on the expectation that rents can be captured before new knowledge has permeated to competitors. The introduction and distribution of goods, which are 'new' as a result of innovations or discoveries that have temporarily given their producers an economic advantage, is particularly difficult in Japan. Obstacles in the distribution system, for example, slow down the pace of introduction and restrain sales volumes while technology rapidly permeates to locals, who hasten to learn in order to launch their own variants in the market. This points to the need to find ways to enable efficient Western firms to expand those activities which they are good at. This contrasts with the demand for market shares for foreigners in computer chips or foreign car components, where foreign firms have already lost their advantage.

Cooperation rather than confrontation

When there are different and partly conflicting interests there may be every reason to advocate one's own position. Economic transactions and contracts do not generally amount to a zero sum game, but both parties ought to profit from voluntary agreements. This is the basic argument why free trade and competition is in everybody's interest. At the same time, all economic activities require a cooperative element.

Governments are in a position to reduce distortions in the operation of business activities across national boundaries (as in the case of the bureaucratic obstacles to trade within the EC). While they may similarly facilitate interactions, for example by removing rigid standards and lack of knowledge such as that prevailing between Europeans and East Asians, they neither can nor should enforce them. Meaningful partnership stems from the realization of mutual gains, and a commitment on both sides to fulfil it within certain, specified realms.

Another problem is that contracting parties may benefit from a deal established in the absence of somebody who is not there to defend his or her interests.[6] This applies to consumers in many trade negotiations. It also applies to the environmental field, where externalities occur outside the market system, enabling short-term fortunes to be earned from the squandering of much larger long-term values. Similar to the management of the multilateral trade system, it will take common international efforts to handle the global environment. Major reductions in CO_2 emissions, for example, would involve multi-million investments, and real action requires initiative and leadership.

157

Similar to the case of trade policies, the United States has so far adopted a defensive position with respect to environmental concerns. Western Europe and especially Japan have well-educated populations that are crowded together in limited areas, and enjoy technological advantages in the handling of environmental concerns. Because of the situation in neighbouring Eastern Europe, Western Europe has become more aware of the need for international solutions. It has been noted that Japan has also declared its ambition to adopt a leading position in regard to international environmental problems.

A mutual commitment in Europe and Japan to lead the way would open up a new area for beneficial exchange. So far, such intentions have not gone much beyond words. Japan and the EC, for example, are the dominating importers of tropical timber. Thereby, they carry a major responsibility for the depletion of biological diversity on earth and the risk of a serious destabilization of the climate. The new Administration in the White House opens up opportunities for Europe and Japan to reverse this record.

Handling human resources

The major lessons from East Asia's performance concern the importance of human resources. The human work force is the crucial competitive factor in today's technologically and economically sophisticated world. At the same time, there are typically imperfections in the capital markets which prevent people from borrowing against future income to finance an education. Investment in human abilities can also be expected to benefit others in addition to the individual. Empirical studies, such as that of Psacharopoulos (1985), demonstrate high social rates of return from education, particularly in developing countries. In this field, Europe may now be in a better position than the United States, which has widely spread problems with illiteracy and basic skills among the general public. The Japanese, however, are far ahead. The Koreans are almost possessed by education and training. To match the emerging competition of highly skilled work forces in East Asia, it is essential that the European educational systems improve and rise to higher standards.

Beyond education in the traditional sense, however, we should pay more attention to the interplay between individuals. Cultural factors play a role in this context, and management must not go against culture. Within the boundaries laid out by each individual society, however, progress in industrial organization as well as social welfare will hinge on our ability to synchronize human efforts. Learning to cooperate among fellow citizens and across national boundaries goes hand in hand.

NOTES

1 CHALLENGES OF A NEW ERA

1 The Asian newly industrialized economies are the Republic of Korea, Taiwan, Hong Kong, and Singapore. These are popularly referred to as the four 'tigers' or 'dragons'. Excluding Singapore, the Association of South-East Asian Nations consists of Thailand, Malaysia, Indonesia, the Philippines and the small Sultanate of Brunei.
2 In 1986, almost 35 per cent of the world's total trade was of the intra-area kind (International Monetary Fund, 1988). Preferential trading arrangements negotiated on a regional basis now affect more of world exports than the Generalized System of Preferences (GSP).

2 THE SHIFT IN GRAVITY

1 OPEC stands for the Organization of Petroleum Exporting Countries.
2 OECD is the Organization for Economic Cooperation and Development, whose members are all the industrialized countries.
3 Import penetration ratio indicates the share of apparent domestic consumption, i.e. domestic production plus imports less exports.
4 See *Economist* (1992).
5 In relative terms, the deficits have mostly been larger for the EC than for the United States (Andersson 1993).
6 See, for example, Nurkse (1952) and Prebish (1962).
7 Smith and Venables (1988) argue that mutual dumping by oligopolistic European firms on each other's segmented markets has contributed to a strong increase in intra-European trade.

3 INTERNATIONALIZATION OF CORPORATE ACTIVITIES AND EAST ASIAN SOCIETIES

1 A commonly used limit for direct investment is 10 per cent of the equity in a firm. Nowadays reference is sometimes made to 'transnational' or 'global' firms. These concepts imply that firms have become international

160

in a true sense, i.e. they have ceased to view their country of origin as 'home' and other countries as 'hosts'. Although there are cases when firms move their headquarters elsewhere, even firms with affiliates in many countries tend to retain a good deal of their national characteristics.

2 See, for example, Dosi (1988).

3 See Andersson *et al.* (1992) for some empirical evidence.

4 As of the mid-1980s, firms from the United States, Germany and Switzerland on average have some nine-tenths of their total R&D located at home, while the corresponding figure for Japan is reported to be 99 per cent (Imai 1993). For Swedish multinational firms, the share located abroad expanded from 13 per cent in 1986 to 16 per cent in 1990 (Andersson 1992a). A general increase in the share located abroad has also been reported by the United Nations (1992).

5 In the terminology of Cooper and John (1988), this can be referred to as 'strategic complementarities'. Knickerbocker (1973) and Vernon (1983) have already noted that markets may be entered by groups of competing firms, i.e. by either 'none' or 'all' rivals. Today, the rivalry is principally associated with the advancement of, and access to, new technologies.

6 See, for example, Romer (1986, 1990), Lucas (1988) and Barro and Sala-i-Martin (1992).

7 This is not shown in the table because of the greater difficulties in comparing educational systems at the university level.

8 Japanese master courses have about as many students in engineering as in natural sciences, while the ratio is only about 1 to 5 in the United States.

9 Corresponding figures are not available in these countries for more recent years, but the pattern is not likely to have changed much over time.

10 Leibenstein (1984) identified the following key characteristics of the Japanese 'management style': consensus formation, spirit of harmony, linking of the welfare of the worker with the well-being of the company, and the lifetime-employment ideal. In comparison with the United States, Japan would also offer a better mix of non-monetary rewards.

11 Using purchasing power parity – a yen rate of 208 to the dollar – the Japan Productivity Center reported in September 1992 that Japan was ninth among industrialized countries in labour productivity as of 1989. The United States had 30 per cent higher productivity. A number of American economists came to similar conclusions. Using spot exchange rates instead, MITI found that Japan leads other industrialized countries in productivity by a significant margin.

12 The liberalization of the credit markets and low interest rates led to an enormous expansion of international credit and currency markets and sky-rocketing equity values in the 1980s.

13 Incidentally, land reform was possible due to the breakdown of the old power structures by intervention from outside.

14 Information is provided by both public and private institutions, including the Japanese Chamber of Commerce, JETRO, Keidanren, MITI and private banks.

15 The Japanese flows are exaggerated partly because they are based on approval or notified rather than actually implemented investments. The stocks of Japanese direct investment are calculated as aggregate flows, accounting for a downward bias since reinvested profits are not included.
16 Imai (1993) analyses the extent to which various corporate activities hinge on the special conditions in Japan, and to what extent they can be internationalized.
17 As always, there are well known exceptions, such as brandy, whisky and perfumes where 'conspicuous consumption' clearly gives rise to abnormal price responses.

4 CONFLICTING TRADE POLICIES

1 According to the judicial Committee of the Senate, 1.1 million assaults on women were registered in the United States in 1991. The real number was said to be perhaps three times as high. This means that several per cent of all American women were attacked in a single year, most of them by their male acquaintances.
2 The differences between Western countries recorded in Table 4.1 must be handled with caution due to the difficulties in comparing national data of this kind.
3 A conference arranged by the National Bureau of Economic Research and the Centre for Economic Policy Research (CEPR) to explore the empirical aspects of strategic trade policy warned about the consequences of applying it (*CEPR Bulletin* 1989).
4 All of Western Europe provided 44 per cent in that year. See Department of Commerce (1992) for direct investment data on a historical cost basis as well as yearly flows.
5 Supplementing provisions were added in 1979, requiring the agreement of existing local merchants before large retailers can open a new outlet.
6 By allowing a greater number of countries to develop, international trade increases the net pool of R&D resources (e.g. money and researchers). To the extent that countries such as Taiwan and Korea advance to the technological frontier, there will be even more noticeable competition for leadership in 'high tech'. Japan's advancement has already released such efforts on a large scale in the United States and Europe.
7 This would not pose any problem with complete property rights and perfect capital markets. As is well known, neither prevail in practice, and the supply of foreign exchange to developing countries is severely constrained.
8 See, for example, Okita (1990).

5 THE THIRD LEG OF THE TRIANGLE

1 Several researchers have argued that the peak in intra-industry trade occurred already in the 1980s, or is on its way (Globerman and Dean 1990; Greenaway and Hine 1991).

2 The prices at which expanding sectors attract factors of production need not reflect social values because of imperfect competition. Helpman and Krugman (1985) presented conditions under which more competition would increase welfare under such circumstances.

3 The EC has allocated more than US$16 billion to five major projects, e.g. ESPRIT, RACE and EUREKA. An additional 'Framework Programme' adopted for 1990–4 receives some US$7 billion.

4 The so-called 'reciprocity clause' probably speeded the establishment of American and Japanese subsidiaries in Europe before coming into effect in 1993. It may also have stimulated financial liberalization in the United States and Japan, but that was unquestionably coming anyway.

5 If outcomes really enhance welfare, it should always be possible to compensate those who have their interests violated. On the other hand, one cannot afford a situation in which compensation is required as soon as the status quo is affected.

6 See Casella (1990) or Bovenberg et al. (1990).

7 Pearce and Sutton (1986).

8 The share of Japanese direct investment flows in the total varies from, for example, about 10 per cent in the UK as of 1986–8 and some 3–4 per cent in France (Kume and Totsuka 1991).

9 See, for example, JETRO (1990b), Dunning and Cantwell (1989), Kume and Totsuka (1991), Narula and Gugler (1991), Thomsen and Nicolaides (1991).

10 It has not been settled whether direct investment substitutes for or expands exports from home. Kume and Totsuka (1991) argue that there is a substitution effect in the case of Japanese direct investment in Europe. The outcome is likely to depend on the interplay between firms and the policies pursued in the host countries, however, with the latter influencing what can be exported in the absence as well as presence of direct investment.

11 This could explain the negative relationship between protectionism and direct investment observed by Orr (1975). See Ellingsen and Wärneryd (1992) for a formal analysis.

12 Local content rules force foreign firms to buy a certain proportion of their input locally.

13 Two students at the Stockholm School of Economics, Ulf Colliander and Håkan Hellström, deserve credit for contributing to these observations.

14 See, for example, Guisinger (1985).

6 POLICY IMPLICATIONS

1 See Kester (1990) and Bank of Japan (1992).

2 See Brodie (1974: 448), or Kelly and Harbison (1970: 205).

3 28 February 1989.

4 Cultural exchange programmes are organized at a bilateral rather than Community level.

5 Bartlett and Ghoshal (1990) recommend that firms establish fora which

promote interactive learning processes between activities in separate regions. One can think of many possible methods to spur similar insights.

6 Deutsch (1958) reported observations that mutual trust between two parties is easier to establish when they are both adversely inclined towards a third part.

REFERENCES

Abegglen, J. and Stalk, G., 1985, *Kaisha, The Japanese Corporation*, Basic Books, New York.

Adelman, I., 1977, 'Redistribution Before Growth – A Strategy for Developing Countries', Inaugural Lecture, Leiden University.

van Agt, A., 1993, 'Europe–Japan: Conflict or Cooperation?', in Andersson, T. (ed.), *Japan: A European Perspective*, Macmillan, London, pp. 3–10.

Aliber, R.Z., 1970, 'A Theory of Direct Foreign Investment', in Kindleberger, C.P. (ed.), *The International Corporation: A Symposium*, MIT Press, Cambridge, MA.

Anderson, K., 1991, 'Europe 1992 and the Western Pacific Countries', *Economic Journal* 101, pp. 1538–52.

Andersson, T., 1991a, *Multinational Investment in Developing Countries*, a Study of Nationalization and Taxation, Routledge, London.

Andersson, T., 1991b, 'Government Failure – the Cause of Global Environmental Mismanagement', *Ecological Economics* 4, pp. 215–36.

Andersson, T., 1992a, 'De Multinationella Företagen, Sverige och EG', Working Paper 323, Industrial Institute for Economic and Social Research, Stockholm.

Andersson, T., 1992b, 'Approaches to Partnerships Causing Asymmetries between Japan and the West', Working Paper 320, Industrial Institute for Economic and Social Research, Stockholm.

Andersson, T., 1992c, 'Investment asymmetry between Europe and Japan', mimeo, Bank of Japan.

Andersson, T. (ed.), 1993, *Japan: A European Perspective*, Macmillan, London.

Andersson, T. and Burenstam Linder, S., 1991, 'Japanese Direct Investment and East Asian Development', in Hansson, G. (ed.), *International Trade and Economic Development*, Routledge, London.

Andersson, T., Arvidsson, N. and Svensson, R., 1992, 'Reconsidering the Choice between Takeover and Greenfield Operations', Working Paper 342, Industrial Institute for Economic and Social Research, Stockholm.

Aoki, M., 1988, *Information, Incentives, and Bargaining in the Japanese Economy*, Cambridge University Press, Cambridge.

Aoki, M., 1990, 'Toward an Economic Model of the Japanese Firm', *Journal of Economic Literature* 28, pp. 1–27.

REFERENCES

Appleby, C. and Bessant, J., 1987, 'Adapting to Decline: Organizational Structures and Government Policy in the UK and West German Foundry Sectors', in Wilks, S. and Wright, M. (eds), *Comparative Government–Industry Relations*, Oxford University Press, Oxford, pp. 181–210.

Arrow, K.J., 1969, 'The Organization of Economic Activity: Issues Pertinent to the Choice of Market Versus Nonmarket Allocation', in *Analysis and Evaluation of Public Expenditures: The PPB System*, vol. 1, U.S. Joint Economic Committee, 91st Congress, US Government Printing Office, Washington, DC, pp. 59–73.

Arrow, K.J., 1974, *The Limits of Organization*, W.W. Norton, New York.

Asanuma, B., 1988, 'Japanese-Supplier Relationships in International Perspective: The Automobile Case', Working Paper 8, Kyoto University, Kyoto.

Asanuma, B., 1989, 'Manufacturer–Supplier Relationship in Japan and the Concept of Relation-Specific Skill', *Journal of Japanese and International Economies* 3, pp. 1–30.

Asian Development Bank, 1990, *Asian Development Outlook*, Manila.

Asian Development Bank, 1991, *Asian Development Outlook*, Manila.

Axelrod, R., 1984, *The Evolution of Cooperation*, Basic Books, New York.

Azariadis, C. and Drazen, A., 1990, 'Threshold Externalities in Economic Development', *Quarterly Journal of Economics* 105, pp. 501–26.

Balassa, B., 1991, *Economic Policies in the Pacific Area Developing Countries*, Macmillan, London.

Bank of Japan, 1992, 'Analysis of Recent Changes in the Relationship between Banks and Corporations Based on Financial Data of Corporations', Special Paper 217, Tokyo.

Barro, R.J. and Sala-i-Martin, X., 1992, 'Convergence' *Journal of Political Economy* 100, pp. 223–51.

Bartlett, C. and Ghoshal, S., 1990, 'Managing Innovation in the Transnational Corporation', in Bartlett, C.A., Doz, Y. and Hedlund, G. (eds), *Managing the Global Firm*, Routledge, London.

Begg, I., 1989, 'European Integration and Regional Policy', *Oxford Review of Economic Policy* 5, pp. 90–104.

Bergsten, C.F., 1991, 'Commentary: The Move Towards Free Trade Zones', in *Policy Implications of Trade and Currency Zones*, Federal Reserve Bank of Kansas City, pp. 43–57.

Bergsten, C.F., Horst, T. and Moran, T., 1978, *American Multinationals and American Interests*, Brookings Institution, Washington, DC.

Bhagwati, J., 1988, *Protectionism*, MIT Press, Cambridge, MA.

Bhagwati, J., 1989, 'U.S. Trade Policy Today', *World Economy*, December.

Bhagwati, J., 1991, *The World Trading System at Risk*, Princeton University Press, Princeton, NJ.

Bovenberg, L., Kremers, J.J.M. and Masson, P.R., 1990, 'Economic and Monetary Union in Europe and Constraints on National Budgetary Policies', IMF Working Paper, Washington, DC.

Brander, J.A. and Spencer, B.J., 1985, 'Export Subsidies and International Market Share Rivalry', *Journal of International Economics* 18, pp. 83–100.

Brodie, F.M., 1974, *Thomas Jefferson*, Bantam Books, Toronto.

Buckley, P.J. and Casson, M., 1976, *The Future of the Multinational Enterprise*, Macmillan, London.

Buigues, P. and Goybet, P., 1989, 'The Community's Industrial Competitiveness and International Trade in Manufactured Products', in Jacquemin, A. and Sapir, A. (eds), *The European Internal Market*, Oxford University Press, New York, pp. 227–47.

Casella, A., 1990, 'Participation in a Currency Region', Working Paper 3220, National Bureau of Economic Research, Cambridge, MA.

Casson, M., 1990, *Enterprise and Competitiveness*, Oxford University Press, New York.

Caves, R.E., 1971, 'International Corporations: The Industrial Economics of Foreign Investment', *Economica* 38, pp. 1–27.

Caves, R.E., 1982, *Multinational Enterprise and Economic Analysis*, Cambridge University Press, Cambridge.

Cawson, A., Holmes, P. and Stevens, A., 1987, 'The Interaction between Firms and the State in France: The Telecommunications and Consumer Electronics Sectors', in Wilks, S. and Wright, M. (eds), *Comparative Government–Industry Relations*, Oxford University Press, Oxford, pp. 10–34.

Cecchini, P., 1988, *The European Challenge 1992, The Benefits of a Single Market*, Wildwood House, Aldershot.

CEPR Bulletin, 1989, 35, October, Centre for Economic Policy Research, London.

Chen, J.A., 1992, 'Japanese Firms with Direct Investments in China and Their Local Management', in Tokunaga, S. (ed.), *Japan's Foreign Investment and Asian Economic Interdependence*, University of Tokyo Press, Tokyo.

Cheshire, P.C., 1990, 'Explaining the Recent Performance of the European Community's Major Urban Regions', *Urban Studies* 27, pp. 311–33.

Clark, K.B., Chew, W.B. and Fujimoto, T., 1987, 'Product Development in the World Auto Industry', *Brookings Papers on Economic Activity*, pp. 729–71.

Coase, R.H., 1937, 'The Nature of the Firm', *Economica* 4, pp. 386–405.

Commission of the European Communities, 1989, *Employment in Europe 1989*, Office of Official Publications of the European Communities, Luxembourg.

Committee for the Study of Economic and Monetary Union, 1989, *Report on Economic and Monetary Union in the European Community* (Delors Report), Office of Official Publications of the European Communities, Luxembourg.

Cooper, R. and John, A., 1988, 'Coordinating Coordination Failures in Keynesian Models', *Quarterly Journal of Economics* 103, pp. 441–63.

Costanza, R., 1992, 'Three Things We Can Do to Achieve Sustainability', mimeo, Maryland.

Coulbeck, N.S., 1984, *The Multinational Banking Industry*, Croom Helm, London.

Daly, H.E., 1968, 'On Economics as a Life Science', *Journal of Political Economy* 76, pp. 392–406.

Denison, E.F., 1962, *Sources of Economic Growth in the United States*, Committee for Economic Development, Washington, DC.

Department of Commerce, 1992, *Survey of Current Business* 3, Washington, DC.

Deutsch, M., 1958, 'Trust and Suspicion', *Journal of Conflict Resolution* 2, pp. 265–79.

Dore, R., 1973, *Japanese Factory – British Factory: The Origins of National Diversity in Industrial Relations*, University of California Press, Los Angeles.

Dosi, G., 1988, 'Sources, Procedures and Microeconomic Effects on Innovation', *Journal of Economic Literature* 26, 1120–71.

Dunning, J.H., 1977, 'Trade, Location of Economic Activity and the MNE: A Search for an Eclectic Approach', in Ohlin, B., Hesselborn, P.-O. and Wijkman, P.M. (eds), *The International Allocation of Economic Activity: Proceedings of a Nobel Symposium Held at Stockholm*, Macmillan, London, pp. 395–418.

Dunning, J.H., 1990, *The Globalization of Firms and Competitiveness of Countries*, Crafoord Lecture, Institute of Economic Research, Lund University.

Dunning, J.H. and Cantwell, J.A., 1989, 'Japanese Manufacturing Direct Investment in the EEC, post 1992: Some Alternative Scenarios', Discussion Paper 132, Department of Economics, University of Reading.

Economic Development Authority, 1984, *Updated Philippine Development Plan, 1984–87*, Manila.

Economist, 1992, 'When China Wakes', November 28, p. 70.

Eliasson, G., Fölster, S., Lindberg, T., Pousette, T. and Taymaz, E., 1990, *The Knowledge Based Information Economy*, Industrial Institute for Economic and Social Research, Stockholm.

Ellingsen, T. and Wärneryd, K., 1992, 'Foreign Direct Investment and the Political Economy of Protectionism', mimeo, Stockholm School of Economics.

Emerson, M., 1988, *The Economics of 1992*, Oxford University Press, Oxford.

Encarnation, D., 1992, *Rivals Beyond Trade: America versus Japan in Global Competition*, Cornell University Press, Cornell.

Europa, 1991, *The Europa World Year Book*, Europa Publications, Rochester.

Europa, 1992, *The Europa World Year Book*, Europa Publications, Rochester.

European Community, 1972, *Structure of Earnings in Industry*, Office of Official Publications of the European Communities, Luxembourg.

Eurostat, 1984, *External Trade and Balance of Payments 1958–83*, Bruxelles/Luxembourg.

Eurostat, 1987, *External Trade and Balance of Payments*, Bruxelles/Luxembourg.

Eurostat, 1989, *External Trade and Balance of Payments*, Bruxelles/Luxembourg.

Eurostat, 1992, *External Trade and Balance of Payments*, Bruxelles/Luxembourg.

Feldman, R.A., 1990, 'The Future of Japanese Banking', in Goodhart, C.A.E. and Sutija, G. (eds), *Japanese Financial Growth*, Macmillan, London.

REFERENCES

Ferguson, C.H., 1988, 'Voodoo Economics', *Harvard Business Review* 66, pp. 55–62.

Friedman, D. and Fung, K.C., 1992, 'Evolutionary Games, Organizational Modes and International Trade Theory', mimeo, University of California, Santa Cruz.

Galenson, W., 1992, *Labor and Economic Growth in Five Asian Countries, South Korea, Malaysia, Taiwan, Thailand, and the Philippines*, Praeger, New York.

Geroski, P., 1988, 'Competition and Innovation', in *Research on the Cost of Non-Europe*, vol. 2, EC Commission, Brussels.

Gilpin, R., 1975, *U.S. Power and the Multinational Corporation*, Basic Books, New York.

Globerman, S. and Dean, J., 1990, 'Recent Trends in Intra-Industry Trade and Their Implications for Future Trade Liberalization', *Weltwirtschaftliches Archiv* 126, pp. 25–49.

Greenaway, D. and Hine, R.C., 1991, *Intra-Industry Specialization, Trade Expansion and Adjustment in the European Economic Space*, vol. 1, Pion, London, pp. 115–34.

Grossman, G.M., 1981, 'The Theory of Domestic Content Protection and Content Preference', *Quarterly Journal of Economics*, November, pp. 583–603.

Grossman, G.M. and Helpman, E., 1990, 'The "New" Growth Theory', *American Economic Review* 80, 2, pp. 86–91.

Guisinger, S., 1985, *Investment Incentives and Performance Requirements*, Praeger, New York.

Gupta, K.L. and Islam, M.A., 1983, 'Foreign Capital, Savings and Growth', Reidel, Boston.

Hamel, G., Doz, Y. and Prahald, C.K., 1986, 'Strategic Partnerships: Success or Surrender?', Working Paper 24, Centre for Business Strategy, London Business School.

Han, S.-T., 1992, *European Integration: The Impact on Asian Newly Industrialized Economies*, OECD, Paris.

Hancher, L. and Reute, M., 1987, 'Legal Culture, Product Licensing, and the Drug Industry', in Wilks, S. and Wright, M. (eds), *Comparative Government–Industry Relations*, Oxford University Press, Oxford, pp. 148–80.

Hawkins, R. and Gladwin, T.N., 1980, 'Conflicts in the International Transfer of Technology: A U.S. Home-Country View', in Sagafi-Nejad, T. and Belfield, R. (eds), *Controlling International Transfer Trilogy*, Pergamon, New York, Chapter 8.

Hedlund, G., 1993, 'Barriers to Market Penetration through Foreign Direct Investment in Japan: An Empirical Analysis of Swedish Firms' Experience 1982–1991', in Andersson, T. (ed.), *Japan: A European Perspective*, Macmillan, London, pp. 77–93.

Helpman, E. and Krugman, P., 1985, *Market Structure and Foreign Trade*, MIT Press, Cambridge, MA.

Hillman, A.L. and Ursprung, H.W., 1992, 'The Political Economy of Interactions between Environmental and Trade Policies', in Anderson,

REFERENCES

K. and Blackhurst, R. (eds), *The Greening of World Trade Issues*, Harvester Wheatsheaf, New York, pp. 195–220.

Hindley, B., 1988, 'Dumping and the Far East Trade of the European Community', *World Economy*, December.

von Hippel, 1987, 'Cooperation between Rivals: Informal Know-How Trading', *Research Policy* 16, pp. 291–302.

Hollander, A., 1987, 'Content Protection and Transnational Monopoly', *Journal of International Economics* 23, pp. 283–97.

Hoshi, T., Kashyap, A. and Scharfstein, D., 1991, 'Corporate Structure, Liquidity, and Investment: Evidence from Japanese Industrial Groups', *Quarterly Journal of Economics* 106, pp. 33–60.

Hymer, S.H., 1960, 'The International Operations of National Firms: A Study of Direct Foreign Investment', Ph.D. dissertation, Massachusetts Institute of Technology.

Imai, K.-I., 1990, 'Japanese Business Groups and the Structural Impediments Initiative', in Yamamura, K. (ed.), *Japan's Economic Structure: Should It Change?*, Society for Japanese Studies, Seattle.

Imai, K.-I., 1993, 'Globalization and Cross-Border Networks of Japanese Firms', in Andersson, T. (ed.), *Japan: A European Perspective*, Macmillan, London, pp. 95–120.

Industrial Bank of Japan, 1991, *Current Issues in International Finance*, March.

International Herald Tribune, 1990a, March 5, Rome.

International Herald Tribune, 1990b, March 6, Rome.

International Monetary Fund, 1988, 'Issues and Developments in International Trade Policy', Occasional Paper 63, Washington, DC.

International Monetary Fund, 1989, *International Financial Statistics*, New York.

International Monetary Fund, 1991, *International Financial Statistics*, New York.

International Monetary Fund, 1992, *International Financial Statistics*, New York.

International Monetary Fund, *Direction of Trade Statistics*, various issues, New York.

International Trade Centre (ITC), UNCTAD/GATT, 1992, 'Recent Patterns and Perspectives in Trade between East Asia and Western Europe', Research Paper No. 1, Geneva.

International Tropical Timber Organization (ITTO), 1991, 'Pre-project Report on Incentives in Producer and Consumer Countries to Promote Sustainable Development of Tropical Forests', Prepared by the Oxford Forestry Institute in Association with the Timber Research and Development Association, Oxford.

INTERPOL (Internationale de Police Criminelle Organisation), 1992, *International Crime Statistics*, Lyon.

Ito, M., 1989, 'Kigyokankankei to Keizokutekitorihiki', in Imai, K. and Komiya, R. (eds), *Nippon no Kigyo*, University of Tokyo Press, Tokyo.

Ito, M., Kiyono, K., Okuno-Fujiwara, M. and Suzumura, K., 1991, *Economic Analysis of Industrial Policy*, Academic Press, San Diego.

Japan Times, 1992, 'When Even Words Fail', October 13, p. 20.

Jensen, M.C., 1989, 'Eclipse of the Public Corporation', *Harvard Business Review* 5, pp. 61–75.

JETRO, 1990a, *The Challenge of the Japanese Market, How 144 Foreign-affiliated Companies Succeeded*, Tokyo.

JETRO, 1990b, *Current Situation of Business Operations of Japanese-Manufacturing Enterprises in Europe – the 6th Survey Report*, Tokyo.

Johnson, C., 1982, *MITI and the Japanese Miracle: The Growth of Industrial Policy, 1925–1975*, Stanford University Press, Stanford, CA.

Kanemoto, Y. and MacLeod, W.B., 1989, 'Optimal Labor Contracts with Non-contractible Human Capital', *Journal of the Japanese and International Economies* 4, pp. 385–402.

Kelly, A.H. and Harbison, W.A., 1970, *The American Constitution*, W.W. Norton, New York.

Keohane, R.O. and Nye, J.S., 1977, *Power and Interdependence: World Politics in Transition*, Little, Brown, Boston.

Kester, W.C., 1990, *Japanese Takeovers: The Global Contest for Corporate Control*, Harvard Business School Press, Cambridge, MA.

Kindleberger, C., 1969, *American Business Abroad: Six Lectures on Direct Investment*, Yale University Press, New Haven, CT.

Knickerbocker, F.T., 1973, *Oligopolistic Reaction and Multinational Enterprise*, Harvard University Press, Cambridge, MA.

Kogut, B., 1985, 'Designing Global Strategies: Comparative and Competitive Value Added Chains', *Sloan Management Review* 26, Summer, pp. 15–28.

Koike, K., 1984, 'Skill Formation Systems in the US and Japan: A Comparative Survey', in Aoki, M. (ed.), *The Economic Analysis of the Japanese Firm*, North-Holland, Amsterdam.

Koike, K., 1988, *Understanding Industrial Relations in Modern Japan*, Macmillan, London.

Kojima, K., 1973, 'A Macroeconomic Approach to Foreign Direct Investment', *Hitotsubashi Journal of Economics* 14, pp. 1–21.

Komiya, R., 1975, 'Planning in Japan', in Bornstein, M. (ed.), *Economic Planning: East and West* , Ballinger, New York, pp. 189–227.

Komiya, R. and Irie, K., 1990, 'The U.S.–Japan Trade Problem: An Economic Analysis from a Japanese Viewpoint', in Yamamura, K. (ed.), *Japanese Economic Structure: Should It Change?*, Society for Japanese Studies, Seattle, pp. 65–104.

Krugman, P., 1984, 'Import Protection as Export Promotion: International Competition in the Presence of Oligopolies and Economics of Scale', in Kierzowski, H. (ed.), *Monopolistic Competition and International Trade*, Clarendon Press, Oxford, pp. 180–193.

Krugman, P. (ed.), 1986, *Strategic Trade Policy and the New International Economics*, MIT Press, Cambridge, MA.

Krugman, P., 1987, 'Is the Japan Problem Over?', in Sato, R. and Wachtel, P. (eds), *Trade Frictions and Economic Policy, Problems and Prospects for Japan and the United States*, Cambridge University Press, Cambridge.

Kumazaki, M., 1992, 'Lessons from the Deforestation of Southeast Asia's Forests', presented at the 2nd National Congress on Biodiversity, Instituto Florestal, Sao Paulo.

Kume, G. and Totsuka, K., 1991, 'Japanese Manufacturing Investment in the EC: Motivations and Locations', in Sumitomo-Life Research Institute with Masaru Yoshitomi, *Japanese Direct Investment in Europe*, Billing, Avebury, pp. 26–56.

Kuznets, S., 1965, *Economic Growth and Structure – Selected Essays*, London,

Kydland, F.E. and Prescott, E.C., 1977, 'Dynamic Inconsistency: Rules Rather than Discretion: The Inconsistency of Optimal Plans', *Journal of Political Economy* 85, pp. 513–48.

Lall, S. and Streeten, P., 1977, *Foreign Investment, Transnationals and Developing Countries*, Macmillan, London.

Law, C.M., 1991, *Restructuring the Global Automobile Industry*, Routledge, London.

Lawrence, R.Z., 1987, 'Imports in Japan: Closed Markets or Minds?', *Brookings Papers in Economic Activity* 2, pp. 517–44.

Lee, J., Rana, P.B. and Iwasaki, Y., 1986, 'Effects of Foreign Capital Inflows of Developing Countries of Asia', Asian Development Bank Staff Paper 30, Manila.

Lehmann, J.-P., 1992, 'France, Japan, Europe and Industrial Competition: The Automotive Case', *International Affairs* 68.

Leibenstein, H., 1984, 'The Japanese Management System: An X-Efficiency-Game Theory Analysis', in Aoki, M. (ed.), *The Economic Analysis of the Japanese Firm*, North-Holland, Amsterdam.

Levitt, B. and March, J.G., 1988, 'Organizational Learning', *Annual Review of Sociology* 14, pp. 319–40.

Lipsey, R.E., 1992, 'Foreign Direct Investment in the US: Changes over Three Decades', Working Paper 4124, National Bureau of Economic Research, Cambridge, MA.

Lipson, C., 1985, *Standing Guard: Protecting Foreign Capital in the 19th and 20th Centuries*, University of California Press, Berkeley.

Little, I., 1981, 'The Experience and Causes of Rapid Labour Intensive Development in Korea, Taiwan Province, Hong Kong and Singapore; and the Possibilities of Emulation', in Lee, E. (ed.), *Export-led Industrialization and Development*, ILO, Asian Employment Programme, Singapore, pp. 23–47.

Ljungqvist, L., 1992, 'Economic Underdevelopment: The Case of a Missing Market for Human Capital', *Journal of Developing Economics*, forthcoming.

Lucas, R.E., 1988, 'On the Mechanisms of Economic Development', *Journal of Monetary Economics* 22, pp. 3–22.

Luhmann, N., 1979, *Trust and Power*, Wiley, London.

Mansfield, E. and Romeo, A., 1980, 'Technology Transfers to Overseas Subsidiaries by U.S.-Based Firms', *Quarterly Journal of Economics* December, pp. 737–50.

Mansfield, E., Romeo, A., Schwartz, M., Teece, D., Wagner, S. and Brach, P., 1983, 'New Findings in Technology Transfer, Productivity and Development', *Research Management* March–April, pp. 11–20.

Mayes, D.G., 1990, 'Factor Mobility', in El-Agraa, A.M. (ed.), *Economics of the European Community*, 3rd edition, Cambridge University Press, Cambridge.

172

REFERENCES

Messerlin, P.A., 1989, 'The EC Antidumping Regulations: A First Economic Appraisal, 1980–85', *Weltwirtschaftliches Archiv* 125, pp. 563–87.

Ministry of Finance, 1990, *Kokusai Kinyu Kyoku Nenpo*, Tokyo.

Ministry of Finance, 1991, *Kokusai Kinyu Kyoku Nenpo*, Tokyo.

Ministry of International Trade and Industry, 1991, *Successful Foreign-Affiliated Enterprises in Japan*, vol. 2, International Business Affairs Division, January, Tokyo.

Ministry of International Trade and Industry, 1992, 'The Position of Small and Medium Enterprises', mimeo, Tokyo.

Ministry of Labour, various years, *Chingin Kozo Kihonchosa*, Tokyo.

Moran, T.H., 1985, *Multinational Corporations, the Political Economy of Foreign Direct Investment*, Lexington Books, Toronto.

Mowery, D.C., 1992, 'The U.S. National Innovation System: Origins and Prospects for Change', *Research Policy* 21, pp. 125–44.

Myrdal, G., 1944, *An American Dilemma, The Negro Problem and Modern Democracy*, Harper, New York.

Nakane, C., 1970, *Japanese Society*, University of California Press, Berkeley.

Narula, R. and Gugler, P., 1991, 'Japanese Direct Investment in Europe: Structure and Trends in the Manufacturing Industry', Working Paper 19, Institute of International Economics and Management, Copenhagen.

Naya, S., 1990, 'Direct Foreign Investment and Trade in East and Southeast Asia', in Jones, R.W. and Krueger, A.O. (eds), *The Political Economy of International Trade*, Blackwell, Cambridge, MA, pp. 288–312.

Neven, D., 1990, 'Structural Adjustment in European Retail Banking: Some Views from Industrial Organization', in Dermine J. (ed.), *European Banking in the 1990s*, Blackwell, Cambridge, MA.

Newsweek, 1989, October 2.

Nurkse, R., 1952, 'Some International Aspects of the Problem of Economic Development', *American Economic Review* 46.

Oda, H. and Grice, R.G., 1988, *Japanese Banking, Securities and Anti-Monopoly Law*, Butterworths, London.

Odaka, K., 1990, 'Sokusenryoku tositeno Chuto-saiyosha; Shokunou no Ippan-tsuyousei wo megutte', mimeo, Hitotsubashi University, Tokyo.

OECD, 1972, *Overall Trade by Countries*, Paris.

OECD, 1982, *Monthly Statistics of Foreign Trade*, Paris.

OECD, 1987, *Economic Outlook Historical Statistics 1960–1985*, Paris.

OECD, 1988, *The Newly Industrialising Countries, Challenge and Opportunity for OECD Industries*, Paris.

OECD, 1989, *Science and Technology Indicators Report*, Paris.

OECD, 1991, *National Accounts*, Paris.

OECD, 1992a, *Monthly Statistics of Foreign Trade*, Paris.

OECD, 1992b, *Economic Outlook Historical Statistics 1960–1990*, Paris.

OECD, 1992c, *Economic Outlook 51*, Paris.

OECD, *Main Economic Indicators*, various issues.

Okimoto, D., 1988, 'Japan, the Societal State', in Okimoto, D. and Rohlen, T. (eds), *Inside the Japanese System: Readings in Contemporary Society and Political Economy*, Stanford University Press, Stanford, CA.

Okita, S., 1990, 'Approaching the 21st Century: Japan's Role', *Japan Times*, Tokyo.

Okuno-Fujiwara, M., 1993, 'Comments on the Japanese Economic System', in Andersson, T. (ed.), *Japan: A European Perspective*, Macmillan, London, pp. 73–6.

Olson, M., 1982, *The Rise and Decline of Nations*, Yale University Press, New Haven, CT.

Orr, D., 1975, 'The Industrial Composition of US Exports and Subsidiary Sales to the Canadian Market: Comment', *American Economic Review* 65, pp. 230–4.

Osterman, P., 1988, *Employment Futures*, Oxford University Press, New York.

Ozawa, T., 1979, *Multinationalism, Japanese Style*, Princeton University Press, Princeton, NJ.

Page, S., 1991, 'Europe 1992; Views of Developing Countries', *Economic Journal* 101, pp. 1553–66.

Palmeter, N.D., 1989, 'The Capture of the Anti-dumping Law', *Yale Journal of International Law* 14, no. 1.

Pearce, J. and Sutton, J., 1986, *Protection and Industrial Policy in Europe*, Routledge & Kegan Paul, London.

Pigou, A.C., 1932, *The Economics of Welfare*, Macmillan, London.

Porter, M.E., 1986, *Competition in Global Industries*, Harvard University Press, Cambridge, MA.

Porter, M.E., 1992, 'Capital Disadvantage: America's Falling Capital Investment System', *Harvard Business Review* September–October, pp. 65–82.

Prebish, R., 1962, 'The Economic Development of Latin America and its Principal Problems', *Economic Bulletin for Latin America* 7.

Prowse, S.D., 1992, 'The Structure of Corporate Ownership in Japan', *Journal of Finance* 46, pp. 1121–40.

Prusa, T.J., 1992, 'Why Are so Many Antidumping Petitions Withdrawn?', *Journal of International Economics* 33, pp. 1–20.

Psacharopoulos, G., 1985, 'Returns to Education: A Further International Update and Implications', *Journal of Human Resources* 20, pp. 583–604.

Reddy, N.M. and Zhao, L., 1990, 'International Technology Transfer: A Review', *Research Policy* 19, pp. 285–307.

Republic of China, 1989, *Statistical Yearbook*, Taipei.

Republic of China, *Taiwan Statistical Data Book*, Taipei, various issues.

Riedel, J., 1988, 'Economic Development in East Asia: Doing What Comes Naturally?', in Hughes, H. (ed.), *Achieving Industrialization in East Asia*, Cambridge University Press, Cambridge, pp. 1–38.

Romer, P.M., 1986, 'Increasing Returns and Long-Run Growth', *Journal of Political Economy* 94, pp. 1002–37.

Romer, P.M., 1990, 'Endogenous Technological Change', *Journal of Political Economy* 98, pp. S71–S102.

Sachs, J., 1986, 'External Debt and Macroeconomic Performance in Latin America and East Asia', *Brookings Papers in Economic Activity* 2, pp. 523–73.

Saxonhouse, G. and Stern, R.M., 1989, 'An Analytical Survey of Formal and Informal Barriers to International Trade and Investment in the United States, Canada and Japan', in Stern R.M. (ed.), *Trade and*

Investment Relations among the U.S., Canada and Japan, University of Chicago Press, Chicago.

Schoppa, L.J., 1991, *Education Reform in Japan, A Case of Immobilist Politics*, Routledge, London.

Schrader, S., 1991, 'Informal Technology Transfer between Firms: Cooperation through Information Trading', *Research Policy* 20, pp. 153–70.

Schultz, T.W., 1963, *The Economic Value of Education*, Columbia University Press, New York.

Schumpeter, J.A., 1939, *Business Cycles*, vols I and II, McGraw-Hill, New York.

Science & Vie, 1992, 'Rare et Vieux, Donc Aphrodisiaque!', August, pp. 46–7.

Servan-Schreiber, J.-J., 1967, *Le Defi Americain*, Denoel, Paris.

Sheard, P., 1991, 'Delegated Monitoring among Delegated Monitors: Principal–Agent Aspects of the Japanese Main Bank System', presented at the Conference Japan in a Global Economy, Stockholm School of Economics, Stockholm.

Shibuya, H., 1990, 'Europe 1992 and the World Economy: Trade, Direct Investment and Finance', mimeo, Bank of Japan, Tokyo.

Shigehara, K., 1990, 'External Dimension of Europe 1992: Its Effects on the Relationship between Europe, the United States and Japan', presented at the Annual Congress of the European Economic Association in Lisbon, Bank of Japan, Tokyo.

Shinohara, M., 1972, 'Growth and Cycles in the Japanese Economy', Institute of Economic Research, Hitotsubashi University, Tokyo.

Shinohara, M., 1982, *Industrial Growth, Trade and Dynamic Patterns in the Japanese Economy*, University of Tokyo Press, Tokyo.

Smith, A. and Venables, A. J., 1988, 'Completing the Internal Market in the European Community', *European Economic Review* 32, pp. 1501–25.

Song, B.-N., 1990, *The Rise of the Korean Economy*, Oxford University Press, Oxford.

Statistics of Sweden, 1991, *Statistisk Årsbok*, Stockholm.

Stiglitz, J.E., 1987, 'Learning to Learn, Localized Learning and Technological Progress', in Dasgupta, P. and Stonehill, S. (eds), *Economic Policy and Technological Performance*, Cambridge University Press, Cambridge.

Streit, M., 1987, 'Industrial policies for technological change: the case of Germany', in Saunders, C.T. (ed.), *Industrial Policies and Structural Change*, Macmillan, London.

Swedenborg, B., 1979, *The Multinational Operations of Swedish Firms: An Analysis of Determinants and Effects*, Industrial Institute for Economic and Social Research, Stockholm.

Takeo, D., 1973, *The Anatomy of Dependence*, Kodansha, Tokyo.

Thomsen, S. and Nicolaides, P., 1991, *The Evolution of Japanese Direct Investment in Europe, Death of a Transistor Salesman*, Harvester Wheatsheaf, New York.

Trela, I. and Whalley, J., 1988, 'Do Developing Countries Lose from the MFA?', National Bureau of Economic Research Working Paper 2618.

Trevor, M., 1989, 'Japanese Managers and British Staff: A Comparison of Relations and Expectations in Blue-Collar and White-Collar Firms', in

Shibagaki, K. and Tetsuo, A. (eds), *Japanese and European Management: Their International Adaptability*, Tokyo University Press, Tokyo, pp. 164–81.

UNCTC (United Nations Centre on Transnational Corporations), 1983, *Transnational Corporations in World Development*, Third Survey, New York.

UNCTD (United Nations Conference on Trade and Development), 1987, *Handbook of International Trade and Statistics*, New York.

UNCTC (United Nations Centre on Transnational Corporations), 1988, *Transnational Corporations in World Development, Trends and Prospects*, New York.

UNCTD (United Nations Conference on Trade and Development), 1990, *Handbook of International Trade and Statistics*, New York.

UNESCO (United Nations Educational Scientific and Cultural Organization), 1991, *Statistical Yearbook*, New York.

United Nations, 1991, *Compendium of Social Statistics and Indicators 1988*, New York.

United Nations, 1992, *World Investment Report – Transnational Corporations as Engines of Growth*, New York.

United Nations, *International Trade Statistics Yearbook*, New York, various issues.

US Department of Commerce, 1991, *State and Metropolitan Area Data Book*, Washington, DC.

Vernon, R., 1966, 'International Investment and International Trade in the Product Cycle', *Quarterly Journal of Economics* 80, pp. 190–207.

Vernon, R., 1979, 'The Product Cycle Hypothesis in a New International Environment', *Oxford Bulletin of Economics and Statistics* 41, pp. 257–67.

Vernon, R., 1983, 'Organizational and Institutional Responses to International Risk', in Herring, R. J. (ed.), *Managing International Risk*, Cambridge University Press, Cambridge.

Vickery, G., 1986, 'International Flows of Technology – Recent Trends and Developments', *STI Review* 1, pp. 47–83.

Wakasugi, R., 1991, 'Why are Japanese Firms so Innovative in Engineering Technology', *Research Policy* 21, pp. 1–12.

Walter, I., 1972, 'Environmental Control and Patterns of International Trade and Investment: An Emerging Policy Issue', *Banca Nazionale Del Lavoro Quarterly Review* 100, pp. 82–106.

Wells, M., 1992, 'Biodiversity Conservation, Affluence and Poverty: Mismatched Costs and Benefits and Efforts to Remedy Them', *Ambio* 21, pp. 237–43.

Wheeler, D. and Mody, A., 1992, 'International Investment Location Decisions, the Case of US Firms', *Journal of International Economics* 33, pp. 57–76.

Wilkinson, E., 1989, *Japan Versus the West, Image and Reality*, Penguin Books, London.

Williamson, O., 1975, *Markets and Hierarchies: Analysis and Antitrust Implications*, Free Press, New York.

Winter, S.G., 1971, 'Satisfying, Selection and the Innovating Remnant', *Quarterly Journal of Economics* 85, pp. 237–61.

REFERENCES

World Bank, 1983, *World Development Report*, New York.

World Bank, 1989–90, *World Tables*, New York.

World Bank, *World Development Report*, New York, various issues.

World Economy, 1989, 'Statement by Forty Economists on American Trade Policy', 2, pp. 263–6.

Yasui, D.I., von der Osten, B. and Park, S.-J., 1989, 'Japanisches Management in der Bundesrepublik Deutschland', Ergebnisbericht der zweiten Enquete-Untersuchung, Berlin.

Zhongguo Xiangzhe Qiye Bao (*China Township Enterprises Newspaper*), 1992, April 4, p. 3.

INDEX

89; economic policies of 6, 7–8, 26, 43, 46, 53–4, 131, 144; research and development and 24, 119
Goybet, P. 17
'green' concerns 8–9, 43, 72, 94–9, 149, 157–8
Grice, R.G. 68
Grossman, G.M. 86
Gugler, P. 136

Han, S.-T. 126
Hayek, F. von 8
health care 75
Hedlund, G. 67
Helpman, E. 86
Hills, Carla 77
Hindley, B. 127
Hong Kong 19, 35; foreign investment by 59, 60; foreign investment in 57, 59; regional integration and 93
Hoshi, T. 50
human resources 6, 8, 42, 52, 143, 145, 158–9
Hymer, S.H. 38, 43

Imai, K.-I. 51, 148
import substitution 28, 29
India 76
Indonesia 19, 26, 35, 55, 57, 60
information trading 40, 152–3
innovation and invention 39, 51, 64, 74
interest rates 4, 73, 125
international trade see trade
internationalization see foreign direct investment; multinational corporations
intra-firm trade 14
intra-industry trade 14, 108, 117–18
invention and innovation 39, 51, 64, 74
investment see foreign direct investment
Iran 73
Iraq 2
Ireland 4
Italy 18, 131
Ito, M. 51, 69

Japan 3–4, 19, 20; aid programmes of 56–7; economy of 1, 8, 44–52, 67–9, 139–40; environmental concerns in 97, 158; export orientation in 26; foreign investment by 34, 56–9, 61–5, 78, 106, 130–8; foreign investment in 65–70, 106; international policy agenda and 142–59; Pacific regional integration and 92–4; research and development in 24, 33, 51, 64; trade and 15–16, 18, 100–7, 109, 112 (US measures against 7, 33–5, 76, 79, 81–5)
Jefferson, Thomas 144
Jensen, M.C. 50
Johnson, C. 46

Kaifu, Toshiko 81–2
Keohane, R.O. 80–1
Keynes, John Maynard 7
Kindleberger, C. 38, 80
Koike, K. 51
Kojima, K. 59
Komiya, R. 46, 69
Korea 8, 19, 26, 35; foreign investment in 57; industrial and social structure in 53, 54, 55
Krugman, P. 77
Kuwait 2
Kuznets, S. 55
Kydland, F.E. 68

labour market 47–9, 53, 64, 120, 132, 145
Lall, S. 42
land ownership 55
Laos 27
Latin America 1, 3, 27
Lawrence, R.Z. 65
Lehmann, J.-P. 138
liberalization, trade 72, 90–4; gains from 85–90
Lipsey, R.E. 78
Lipson, C. 37, 79
Little, I. 26
Ljungqvist, L. 42
local contest rules 34, 134
Luhmann, N. 49